THE POWER OF BREATH

For love, joy and health

by Devapath

Ten Osho Diamond Breath meditations to enrich your life

Perfect
Publishers Ltd

ISBN 978-1-905399-52-9

Cover Design by Duncan Bamford
http://www.insightillustration.co.uk

Dhyan Prafulla

Edited by Jan Andersen
http://www.creativecopywriter.org

Prem Shunyo, Prem Maitri

PERFECT PUBLISHERS LTD
23 Maitland Avenue
Cambridge
CB4 1TA
England
http://www.perfectpublishers.co.uk

Dedication

In gratitude to my beloved master Osho for guiding me on the inner journey towards love, joy and freedom.

Contents

Preface

There is every possibility that every human being
can become a Gautam Buddha. This is the only way
To save this beautiful planet earth.

Osho

Our breath is like the most beautiful diamond of our life. It
shines its light on our body, mind, heart and spirit to keep
us healthy, loving and joyful. From whatever side we look
into our life, we will find thousands of facets of the
diamond of breath sending waves of light into our
existence.

The power of breath has brought lots of joy and inner
transformation to my own life. That's why this book has
become a little love letter of conscious deep and natural
breathing to the world. Forgive me for my sometimes
overwhelming enthusiasm and excuse me if I am not
always able to tell you in rational terms what I can feel and
experience by the power of deep breathing.

But trust me, it is mind blowing to realise a little more each
day how rich this world of breathing really is. It is amazing
how it can change our life for the better. Truly, for me the
breath is the most forgotten, most powerful and most
valuable diamond of our existence!

It's surprising how limited our understanding of this hidden
treasure really is and I hope this little book can motivate
you to start the great adventure of breathing.

A Fresh Breeze

Breathing is something we all do and all take for granted. It is the primary requisite for living and yet my observation is that most of us breathe in a very shallow way, thus our enjoyment of life is similarly shallow. We learn many things in life but we do not learn the art of breathing, which is needed if we are to enjoy a fulfilling life.

My work is to help people understand the significance of conscious, deep breathing. Correct breathing will alter our whole experience of life. What do I mean by "correct breathing"? By bringing awareness to our breathing we awake the longing to breathe and live more naturally and intensely. We experience a breath that opens the door to the dimensions of both healthy relaxation and a hitherto unknown creativity.

All around I see people stressed out by the enormous challenges of modern life, holding their breath. Being chronically stressed, our breathing is constricted and we feel trapped in the duties of daily life. Somehow, intuitively and with all the best intentions, we try to find ways to release this stress by fitness activities. We long for unlocking our breathing and feel freer.

But without a deeper understanding of our respiration we tend to revert to shallow breathing. Though we can unlock our breathing for a moment in an exercise like jogging, it will get stuck again. Sadly we have learned that we have to repress our strong feelings and only by blocking our breath can we do so. We need shallow breathing to keep our repressions working. As a consequence, we cannot recharge our "batteries" of life energy by a deep breathing anymore.

As a result, we start compensating our leaking of energy by running on willpower. We begin to exhaust ourselves without even recognising that we are doing so. Until one day our body and mind break down and our life loses all colour and creativity. Stuck in a cycle of hyperactivity and restlessness, we are deprived of the profound feelings of relaxation, inner peacefulness and rejuvenating sleep.

Above, I've noted some of the major benefits of correct breathing: Relaxation, replenishment, health, creativity, calmness, connectedness and living at a more profound level. In this little book I will explore these and other benefits of deep breathing in depth and teach ways to remember correct breathing.

A New Quality of Life

Have you ever thought how essential breathing is?

Just imagine that you stop breathing completely. Gradually, you will lose your vibrant aura and your creative energy. You will begin to feel more and more tired and depressed. Life will lose all fascination and your sensitivity, your sexuality, even your desire to move, will all disappear. Soon you will die - first your brain and then the rest of your body. When your last breath leaves you and death comes, your body is left as an empty corpse.

We are not aware that shallow breathing keeps us close to the state of dying - either physically or psychologically - with just enough breath to survive. In fact, we live permanently on the edge of total exhaustion, disease and the collapsing of our life energy. It looks like we are afraid of living.

On the other hand, deep breathing moves us towards a richer state of being and allows us to live the life we long for. Breathing and living life to the fullest; that is, loving our body, enjoying our sexual energies, being creative and expanding our consciousness in meditation.

Another aspect of deep breathing is its ability to improve the quality of our life by teaching us the art of trusting and letting go into the natural course of life. Moving with the spontaneous dance of the breath, we learn to be playful and flexible and to become like children again moved by the winds of existence.

A New Education

No matter what, nothing is worth giving up breathing and feeling the beauty of existence surrounding us. From our first breath to our last breath it allows us to rejoice in the art of living. We need a new kind of education - a life-long education – to help us to recognise, value and polish the diamond of breath and realise our spiritual potential as human beings.

Increasingly in the developed world, the tendency is to curtail our physical activity. In addition, typically, we are discouraged from emotional expression. We need to learn how to release our accumulated physical and emotional tension in order to relax and feel our body's need to breathe deeply again.

This will sharpen our awareness about the way we breathe and the way we live. Giving attention to our breath is nourishing our breath. Experiencing our breath consciously we can see clearly how we stop our own life energy by physical contractions, mental tensions and a closed heart. We can see how we limit the quality of our life by forgetting the most essential – our breath.

To get a positive experience of our breath, let's remember a moment when we were happily breathing. Maybe we were with a beloved or being touched by a beautiful scene in nature, like a sunset. We felt so connected to life and felt so lucky for being part of this pulsing and breathing universe. We felt so liberated and so relaxed, like breathing in inner ecstasy.

Just imagine that through the awareness of our breath we can make this joyful experience available for all of our life. We will be overwhelmed by the truth, intensity and beauty of being connected to the cosmic breath. We will be extremely grateful to be alive.

A New Beginning

Relationships can be rife with tension, arguments, fighting and the inability to understand the other. Deeply relaxed breathing opens the heart, creating a sense of calm, of intimacy and love. So the quality of our breathing will be reflected in our relationships too.

Breathing gives us the energy to open our heart to love. It is time to learn this art because then the world can find a new inner breath. According to the Sufi mystic Rumi, that is what love is, "the inner breath of our being." It will be this that brings back the light, laughter and peacefulness to this tortured planet.

As a doctor, I realised that a heart attack is symptomatic of our stressful, overly controlled and loveless modern lifestyle. As a meditative therapist, I see now, with growing clarity, that a truly fulfilled life depends on our capacity to love – to love others and ourselves. In fact, love is the most powerful healing and relaxing force in our lives.

Missing love, we attack our own heart. We not only attack the rest of the world but also ourselves. We do not breathe and by not breathing deeply we have no energy to grow in love. We need to take a deep breath to overcome our negative attitudes towards life. We need a deep breath to make this earth a paradise.

Bringing awareness to how we breathe and learning to breathe deeply again helps us to realise that such deep breathing cleans, nourishes and vitalises our body, our mind, our heart and our spirit in each moment of our life. In a most profound way existence is taking care of us. Without us even realising it, life is breathing us.

Ultimately we learn that life is not in our hands, but is given to us by existence. One day our breathing will stop and life will be taken away again. Why not enjoy it as long as we have it? Relaxing and trusting the intelligence of our breath will move us beyond our fears and anxieties of life and guide us towards our inner treasures.

With a deep exhalation we can release the mountain of stress we carry around. With a deep inhalation we can breathe into a new beginning in each moment of our life. The next breath will be our opening for love and meditation.

A New Ecology

Sadly, we have learnt to see ourselves being above and separate from nature. That's why we can destroy nature without feeling that it is part of us. We do not realise that hurting nature will also give pain to ourselves. As we breathe the same air, we suffer from the same pollution.

When we are unaware of the value of correct breathing and the nourishment it gives us, we become insensitive to the air that fills our lungs and enables us to enjoy a healthy life. Carelessly and unconsciously we poison the breath of our planet, which is so essential for our wellbeing.

We forget that our planet's oxygen resources are limited and pollute the air by the needs of a growing population. Mother earth cannot digest the pollution by millions of cars, thousands of airplanes, hundreds of rockets, energy plants and forest fires to erode new farmland, or an enormous meat production, which all contribute massively to the greenhouse effect and air poisoning. In addition, we destroy our forests - the green lung of our planet - to create more space for an ever increasing population. It might be no coincidence that at the same time lung cancer is increasing also. As we are exhausted by the demands and the stresses of an overcrowded world, so is nature.

We don't have time to recover and we find less and less beautiful spaces to recover together with nature. We release our stress in stormy relationships and violent waves of little wars, while nature unlashes its stress by hurricanes, typhoons or earthquakes.

Politicians and religious leaders support family programmes to raise the birth rate and the number of their followers. They are not aware how badly this affects the quality of our life because so many people need space, food, water and air to breathe. In the end our children will have to face a devastated planet.

Isn't it time to ask ourselves: For how many people can mother earth provide a good life? Do we really want to go on blindly following our unconscious biological programme of reproduction and threaten the survival of this beautiful blue planet? And what are the alternatives?

Isn't it better to take time out and to learn to become more loving and sensitive to our breath, our body and our feelings? So that we first learn to deeply love ourselves and then we can bring this love to the outer world – to our loved ones, friends, children and nature for the creation of a new, healthy and beautiful world.

A New Womb

If we can feel how poorly we breathe and miss an atmosphere of love around us then naturally we will try everything to save mother earth – and ourselves – from our own destructive hands. Feeling even the smallest change in the quality of air, we will do everything to keep it clean, fresh and nourishing.

Becoming more sensitive to the body and its breath, we will be able to take better care of it. We will "hear" when our body desperately calls for attention due to its over reacting or collapsing immune system and due to a whole range of illnesses, from allergies and infections to cancer and vascular diseases.

The outer world reflects our inner world. Protecting the outer environment needs to go hand in hand with protecting our inner environment. A key is to learn to deal with our growing frustration and negativity in positive ways like active meditation and transformative therapies. Otherwise we are in danger of destroying the last islands of inner and outer beauty.

Working with people now for more than thirty years gives me the impression that our destructiveness with mother earth has its roots already in the prenatal relationship with our mother. First we experience the stress of modern life in the womb and then enter this life in a cold and impersonal birth. The lack of touch and intimacy during our childhood adds another painful mark in our psychology.

Not feeling loved and welcomed from the day we were conceived and finally born, we hold our breath and become afraid of life. We become like babies, freaking out and screaming desperately for the parents to come and take us in their arms, so that we can relax and trust into a deep and calming rhythm of breathing again.

In many ways I see my group therapies today similar to being a healing womb for our physical and emotional wounds from the past. Here the art of breathing plays an exceptionally important role in our transformation. It is a diamond, which brings light to the dark sides of our life and enlightens our body, mind, heart and spirit.

Paradise Now

A new awareness of our breath opens the gate to paradise now. We dream of a better world and we have the potential to create it. By working on ourselves and discovering the many facets of our breath, we can find our inner resources for love, joy and health.

This great adventure might feel sometimes easy and sometimes arduous. Often we might work hard but cannot see the result. Then it might be helpful to remember the way love happens; we desperately look for it, we look for a partner and nothing happens. But just the day we give up and relax, our new love stands in front of us.

So, let's take it easy. Let's play like children and be surprised by the world of breathing. This book will give some help for daily life to develop our own friendship with the diamond of breath. Whenever or wherever we are, it gives us little exercises and meditations to play and grow with our breathing. It offers a map to come back to ourselves and it will not take long to find our own ways to remember our breathing as the treasure house of our being.

A new quality of breathing into life is calling us. From being a physician and working in medicine it has guided me to become a spiritual therapist working with meditation. Over the past few years, I have written the collection of short articles for a widely distributed Chinese health magazine. In this book I have added some personal experiences and stories from the therapy room.

Chapter 1

Breathing with Awareness

There is no need to teach all kinds of meditations; just one method I can choose which can be the simplest, easiest and applicable to all. And just that one method can be spread all over the world. It is what I call witnessing the breath. It is a very simple method.

Osho

The Breath Gives Life

Life gives breath and breath gives life! The most important function for sustaining life is the most forgotten one. Our breath carries not only oxygen, as we learn in western medicine; it also carries the energy of life – *Prana* – as we learn in the healing schools of the East.

The first question from a doctor visiting his patient should be: "How is your breathing?" Similarly, the first question from a psychologist could be: "What hinders you from breathing deeply?" All our psychological problems are related to incorrect breathing patterns. The first question from a family therapist can take the same direction: "Who in the family holds their breath the most?"

That reminds me of a little anecdote: One day the schoolteacher asks the class what kind of medicine they know of and what it is good for. The kids mention aspirin, fish oil and other things, saying that they all support their health. Finally, the smallest one jumps up and screams. "Hey, hey, you have forgotten the most important! It's oxygen, oxygen! They gave it to my grandma!" "And what is it good for?" asks the teacher. "Well, when they starting wheeling it out of her room," the kid says, "she whispered breathlessly, 'Don't take it aw…a….y!'"

There is no better medicine than our breath and, if we take it away, life is immediately finished. This little boy learnt the first lesson of life: Breathing is the key!

Coming Home to the Body - Our Temple

The awareness of our breathing starts with bringing our attention from the outside world back to the temple of our body.

The body is our truth. It is like an innocent child expressing our state of being. Here we can recognise the pathways, the working stations and the vitalising effects of our breath. Just feeling our breath's energy flow gives us a wonderful feeling and opens our eyes to the reality of our body.

Let's remember the feeling we have when a friend gives us loving attention instead of ignoring us. Receiving a loving look, a gentle touch or a supportive word, we are ready to do anything for him. In the same way, when we are loving and supportive towards our body, it is ready to do anything for us.

The body is a luxury container and a wonderful vehicle for our breath. If we look at our body with awareness we know where we are with ourselves. The mind easily can lie and give us a false self-image, which we like to believe, in order to feel good about ourselves and to be accepted in society.

But the body reveals a deeper truth. It cannot lie. Sadly we have forgotten to read its language and to listen to its signals, warning us of dis-ease or asking us for loving support. By detecting these expressions early enough and taking care of our body's imbalances, we can prevent many illnesses.

Our body has a wide spectrum of ways to breathe and balance our life. Exploring them is an exciting and neverending adventure. It brings intensity and many insights about the art of living and enjoying ourselves on the path of life from birth to death.

Life after birth starts with a deep inhalation and rapid breathing to survive and stay alive. It ends, as we move towards death, with the slowing down of our breathing and finally having our last long exhalation. In between, we experience a wide variety of breath frequencies, from fast, therapeutic and active, athletic or sexual and emotional, to a naturally relaxed and ultimately balanced, slow, meditative breathing.

In addition, we can fine-tune our respiration by alternating its intensity through the area, depth and rhythm of our breathing. All these dimensions are interconnected like in a simple activity such as running. First, the breathing deepens, then changes rhythm and finally involves most areas of our body. Something similar occurs when we move into strong emotional expressions.

Through the incredible variety of breathing patterns we can experience life in all its colours. By playing with our breath we can learn to live in harmony with the rhythms of nature again; just as we breathe joyfully, we allow the nature that surrounds us to breathe joyfully too. After all, we need fresh air in order to be healthy.

Refreshing Our Life Energies by Right Breathing

Naturally relaxed breathing gives us the sensitivity and carefulness to support our immediate environment. It allows us to feel and understand nature because we can feel that we are part of it. If all of mankind breathed naturally, intuitively we would keep all of its green areas "breathing" to avoid destroying our own life support.

We would enjoy living in a beautiful, clean world so we would have no interest in harming it in any way. As we care for our own breathing, so we would care for the breath of mother earth.

Our breath is a treasure box for long lasting health, wellbeing and inner transformation. But living in a constant hurry and over-activity we have become insensitive to it. It's worth taking time to feel and to enjoy the power of breathing in order to have a more relaxed and fulfilled life.

Good breathing oxygenates, energises and cleans our body. It cleanses and clears our mind and balances our emotions. This makes it the most important factor in preventive health care and medicine. Let's remember that the many health benefits of physical exercising, such as in sports, dance, Yoga, or Tai Chi, come from the stimulation and balancing of our breath.

From the head to the toes the breath does an amazing job in our body. With each breath oxygen and energy flood into our body and keep it connected to the pulse of life. Just a little awareness can help to open the body-mind to a deeper breath and its healing and enlightening work on our souls.

Breathing on the Spiritual Path

The awareness of our breath is a wonderful teaching on the path of life. It helps us to realise first how close all the dimensions of our being are closely connected; body, mind, heart and spirit are not separate units, but one organic whole being influenced and expressing itself by the way we breathe.

Many of us probably know that our body-mind influences our respiration, but the effect that the state of our spiritual being has on our breathing is mostly unknown. Cited by the mystic Osho, there is a beautiful parable describing our travelling through life from the jungle of our mind to coming home in ourselves.

The jungle man lives in darkness, in total unconsciousness. He doesn't even know that there is another world, a world other than surviving in the jungle of life. His existence is all about protecting himself and securing his life. He is totally identified with his mind, believes whatever it says and gets lost in whatever emotion it triggers.

He is ridden by fear and is absolutely unconscious about what he is doing; and so is his breath. It is contracted and doesn't dare to expand. It is tense and chaotic because it is dominated by the moods of his anxious mind. The jungle man cannot feel in harmony with life because he controls his breath and keeps it as shallow as possible in order not to feel himself and to control nature.

But sometimes he accidentally makes it to lighter areas of life. From the jungle he arrives at the forest, where he finds some more openness and rare rays of light. He becomes unhappy with his safe and well-planned life and has the feeling that there is more to life, but he doesn't know where to go to find it. So he moves here and there without orientation.

Dragged between fear to lose the old and curiosity to find the new, the forest man is in a state of confusion and so is his breath. He breathes the old protected way and begins to feel suffocated by his old life. But in moments when he can see the light on the horizon and his mind relaxes, the breath also gives him an experience of deep tranquillity and easiness. He catches the longing for a richer quality of life.

One day he will find the meditative garden of a spiritual master. The moment he is courageous enough to enter it, he will know that he has arrived at the right place in his life. He settles and becomes a gardener preparing his inner garden of spirituality to grow. His mind begins deeply to relax and so does his breath.

His breathing becomes calmer, fuller and expands into a new depth of his being – the same depth he begins to feel with life. With his breath he begins to feel an innocence, which connects him with the feeling of becoming like a child again.

One day suddenly he feels he has arrived home. He has found his original being. He has come home in existence after lives of feeling lost and separated. His mind becomes like a silent lake and so does his breath. He becomes a silent lake full of existence's most precious energy.

The Breath Awareness Meditation

Now a little breath-awareness exercise to relax and feel our breathing. To prepare, put on your favourite soft music, find a comfortable and silent space in which to sit or lie down and relax. Take a moment to feel your body breathing and to let go of any tensions with your out breath.

In the first stage of the meditation, you will explore your breathing into various spaces of the body and in the second part you will relax into the waves of your breath rolling all over your body.

Stage 1: 10 Minutes

Rub your hands together until they are warm and then gently put them, palm downwards, on your lower belly. If you like you can also gently move your hands softly around your abdomen. Consciously breathe into your belly.

Feel the belly relaxing and the breath deepening. Imagine the belly is an ocean of energy that reaches from the pelvis to the solar plexus - that place where the belly touches the lower ribs. Feel its sensitivity and sensuality. Feel the waves of breathing moving through your belly.

Then let your hands move up until they rest around your solar plexus area. Feel the movement of your breathing and relax. Connect to this sensitive area, which is like a bridge between the lower and the upper body.

Now let your hands wander to the upper chest and allow them to rest on your ribs and the chest bone on top of your heart area. Feel the movement of your breathing touching this vulnerable and well-protected area of the body. Breathe softly and gently. Let the chest expand and be open to the feelings of lovingness and peacefulness from your heart centre.

Finally, bring your hands to the "gate of breathing" where the throat and the neck work closely together with the mouth and the nose to invite the breath. Here, inside the body, the breath touches your thyroid gland, the windpipe, the oesophagus and the spine. Fearful stress keeps this area contracted, but your loving touch and new awareness can bring relaxation and openness to this area.

Stage 2: 10 Minutes

In the second part of the meditation, bring your hands back to your belly and let them rest there. Imagine that the belly is the beginning of your breathing. From here the breath expands into the whole body. Feel your breathing moving like a soft wave through your body.

With the inhalation it moves upwards towards the chest and with the exhalation it moves downwards towards the belly. Feel that life is breathing through you. Feel existence nourishing you with each breath, keeping you alive and joyful.

To end your meditation, take a very deep breath and, as you do so, enjoy the opening of your body to the sensation of life. Inhale deeply and take this beautiful healing force of conscious breathing into your daily life.

Chapter 2

Breathing Beyond Stress

Whenever you feel the mind is not tranquil, tense, worried, chattering, anxiety, constantly dreaming, do one thing: first exhale deeply. With the throwing of the air the mood will be thrown out, because breathing is everything.

Osho

Releasing Stress with a Good Breath

Living in today's busy world is a challenge, a challenge not only in our business life but also our private life. We have to deal with constant stress and conflict, rapid change and a growing insecurity. This places a unique demand on us mentally, physically and emotionally. Solid health, good breathing, awareness, trust and the intuition to respond quickly, effectively and compassionately is needed.

Leadership in our personal and business life requires the ability to be relaxed enough to remain creative. We need to learn the great art of releasing stress to prevent ourselves from, becoming burnt-out and then ill. Releasing stress allows us to stay connected to our strength, to keep our spirits up even in difficult moments, permitting us to move into passionate action with a compassionate heart.

Recently, in a workshop to transform the quality of life, a participant informed the group that he was very successful in business but impotent in being in touch with himself. His children asked him why he had been participating in this process for over a year now. To his own surprise he replied

9

that he wanted to learn to cry again, something he had not been able to do since childhood.

Whenever he returned home from further trainings his children would ask if he was able to cry. To his shame he had to admit no, he could not. In this current workshop with some deep breathing sessions he reconnected with his forgotten ability to enjoy himself. Finally, in a meditation for the heart, he realised his need for love and acceptance and he broke down in tears. He was a different person afterwards.

Overcoming Lethal Stress

Stress has a deep connection to fear; it is essentially the result of the fears and worries of the mind. We are afraid of failure, of not being good enough, of losing, of being judged, rejected or punished. We fight against our emotions as if they are our worst enemy, thus we feel constantly under pressure. In a male-oriented society, it sounds better to say, "I am stressed!" than to say, "I am afraid!" But only when we can learn to face fear and move beyond it will we be able to deeply relax again.

Acute stress as a momentary reaction of our body-mind to a challenging situation is natural. As a protection against the dangers of life, it is accompanied by a series of physiological changes produced by the autonomous nervous system and adrenal glands. This includes increased heart rate, rapid breathing, tenseness or trembling of muscles, increased sweating and dryness of the mouth. In short, the feeling is a state of alarm. The moment the stressful situation disappears, the system swings back to normal, balanced and relaxed.

But stress can also influence our body-mind to the extent of causing permanent health problems. It can become toxic. If we don't take care to regularly release tension, the stress in our body and our mind accumulates and our system moves into a *chronic stress* mode. It does not swing back to normal but stays in an accelerated status of fearful tension. It remains on permanent alarm.

We all know what this means; it means nervousness, over-activity, sleeping problems, a chronic tiredness, irritability, desperation and depression. In such a state we may harm our relationships and we may develop habits of drug abuse in order to escape from our reality.

This tense life becomes unbearable so we may come close to develop cancer, explode in a heart attack or entertain thoughts of suicide. For those who are chronically stressed the world loses all joy and colour. They begin to reach the level of *lethal stress*.

As I have noted, relationships – both personal and professional – can be affected by such stress. They can also provoke it. Recently scientists have discovered that a partner dying or leaving can result in a change from acute stress to chronic stress and finally lethal emotional stress. Often after a period of approximately two years the unreleased stress from this separation might cause cancer or other serious health problems.

I have seen similar reactions in people who have had to overcome painful problems in their work life. A woman who had developed a prestigious project that promised a sizeable income felt deeply betrayed when she lost the job and a former colleague took over the project; she swallowed the pain and soon after developed bone cancer.

Timely stress release is needed for survival and vital for staying healthy!

Why Do We Feel so Easily Stressed?

Often we keep ourselves in permanent stress even though somehow we realise it. But we cannot change the pattern and end up in the same old story over and over again; agitated, exhausted, sleepless and finally sick. Like smoking, we know it's not good for our health but we do it anyway.

Why are we so addicted to stress? There are a number of reasons and many go back to the very beginning of our life, when we were living in a stressful surrounding and our nervous system got "infected" by it.

Let's start with the history of our life and go to the moment when we came into existence? Well, it was the day when our parents enjoyed a deep breath, made love and conceived us in a certain physical, mental, emotional and spiritual state of being with each other. It was not just the egg and the sperm merging into each other to create a new gene pool.

It was an event with a strong energetic atmosphere surrounding it, which has deeply influenced the forming of this new creation, which we became. If conception has not happened in a loving and joyful connection between the parents, it has left us with a deeply unconscious imprint of stressful tensions.

As we developed in our mother's womb, if she was not in the most comfortable, supportive and relaxing circumstances herself, we picked up all her tension. While our body was growing in prenatal life, her stress level programmed our nervous system.

Finally, passing through an extremely threatening and painful birth process has added a great deal to the level of stress we already had received in the preceding months. Let's hope we released it with a good first scream after birth and were then able to relax in the warm arms of our mother. Otherwise we might be haunted by the pains of our birth trauma our whole life.

Growing up as a child and living in a tense family situation with permanent conflicts between parents or other stress factors adds to the conditioning for stress. Being criticised punished or rejected and not feeling the loving support of our parents gave us the feeling that something was wrong with us. For the rest of our lives we will be stressed by a feeling of insecurity about ourselves.

The Addiction to Stress

After all these experiences we are programmed to stress ourselves! We don't feel good enough, intelligent enough or beautiful enough. We always feel that we should be different, better. We are afraid to be ourselves and to express ourselves. We avoid looking at ourselves and need others so we can be distracted from ourselves. This makes it impossible to be alone and in a love affair with ourselves.

This is why we keep our attention outside and we are always running somewhere, for something – anything! We run like an overheated car at top speed until the motor breaks down. We hear that meditation is good for us to relax but we have many excuses not to do it. Nothing can stop us until we collapse in chronic fatigue, or depression.

From early childhood on we learn that laziness is something bad and we also have a similar feeling regarding relaxation. Paradoxically, relaxation becomes stressful. We feel loved and rewarded only if we achieve something extraordinary, through lots of tense effort. The message is: stress is okay because it shows that we are successful. It becomes our second nature. If we are not stressed something is wrong with us.

The "advantage" of stress is that it protects us from feeling ourselves and from being sensitive and vulnerable to the tough and judgmental world around us. Just looking at the amount of stress we carry today, we can see how dangerous we feel this world to be. We have developed a habit to protect ourselves from a hostile world.

Chronic unresolved stress is the shadow of fear – ultimately the fear of dying. A healthy child develops no chronic stress pattern as long as the child is allowed to breathe, move, play and expand in his or her own individual way. But the moment the child is forced to behave differently in order to be loved by his or her parents, out of fear he or she develops a personality to protect his or herself; the child learns to please others in order not to be rejected, to be left alone or ultimately to die of deprivation.

In India there is one word for the fear of time and death: "Kala". If we are afraid of death, we are afraid of time too. We are stressed because we are afraid of losing our time to live and that soon we will die. We are afraid that every day our life is becoming shorter and we are still unfulfilled. We focus our life on safety and get bored instead of living our desires totally and stepping into the insecurity of life. We have not learned the art of living!

Moving Beyond Stress

The Buddha asks us to live in the "here and now". Each moment of intense living allows us to forget our fears and our stresses and to experience life as an ongoing adventure. This is very different from the stressful intensity caused by a fearful mind, which makes many people feel sick today.

It is the intensity of a child enjoying life. It is the intensity of living with a relaxed body and mind and feeling the power and the beauty of life vibrating inside us. Yes, the world might be dangerous sometimes, but our tense mind makes it appear even more dangerous than it really is.

Our tense mind keeps us pushing and fighting, when in fact we could learn to relax even in the greatest storms of life. It generates the fear from which our whole organism is suffering. We hold our breath and contract our body. Instead of enjoying the spirit of love and trust in life, we suffer from a closed heart imprisoned in a rigid way of living.

Stress is not the real problem. It is our over-protective and over-loaded mind, which keeps our body tense and disconnected from the juice of life. It keeps us imprisoned in a world of endless thinking, causing us to fearfully shrink into cancer or angrily explode into a heart attack.

So, the solution is: Stress needs to be addressed in both the body and the mind. For the symptoms of stress to disappear we need to treat the cause in our restless mind, tense body

15

and contracted breathing patterns. We also need to have different life values, which allow us to live intensely and joyfully.

The Dynamic Tension Release Meditation

The moment we learn to live totally, creatively and without our mind's inhibitions, chronic stress patterns will disappear. All fearful tensions can dissolve and be transformed into an experience of easiness and lightness. For millions of people Osho's Active Meditations or other forms of Dynamic Tension Release have opened the door towards wellbeing and to the experience of a new quality of life.

Through these techniques, in a short period of time we regain vitality and clarity; we feel healthy and can enjoy our relationships in more depth. Through deeper breathing, moving and releasing our body from old tensions and learning to connect with others and existence in new ways, our inner resources of energy will awaken. We are able to pass the mountains of stress without jeopardising our health and inner balance.

In fact the true art of modern life is one of transforming stress into an energy, which supports a fulfilling personal and professional life. A wise Chinese mystic said: "Work quietly, silently, untroubled by any idea of success or failure." Now let's get ready to release our stress through a little meditation.

Stage 1: 10 Minutes

In chronic stress, as in fear, the yin and yang of our breath - the exhalation and the inhalation - are out of balance. We hold our breath. We are afraid to exhale completely. We need to learn to exhale deeply again in order to release our stress and balance our respiration. This will also bring harmony to our nervous system.

Stand with loose knees and relax your pelvis, abdomen and spine. Relax your mouth and take some deep breaths to feel and expand your body in all directions – to the front, to the back and to the sides. Be aware of the tensions in different parts of your body.

Over the next few minutes, one by one contract the tensest parts of your body totally and hold your breath. Then exhale strongly with a good sound and shake out all the tensions. Continue with the deep breathing and with the contracting and releasing process.

Stage 2: 10 Minutes

Now sit down for ten minutes, close your eyes and relax. Allow your body to breathe naturally. Feel the different qualities of your inhalation and exhalation. The in-breath brings life and the out-breath brings relaxation. Watch the rhythm of life reflected in each breath. Whenever your mind wanders somewhere else, return to watching and to enjoying your breathing.

Chapter 3

Breathing for Inner Healing

Breath is your life and breath is also the bridge between the conscious and the unconscious, between your body and your soul. This bridge has to be used. If you can use the bridge rightly, you can go to the other shore.

Osho

Sailing in the Winds of Life

Enjoying our natural breathing is like sailing with pleasure in the winds of life. Life is breathing us! Life is moving us and we simply need to learn to allow it. If we can be flexible and trust the changing winds of life they will carry us to wherever existence wants to bring us. Learning the art of breathing is like becoming a skipper who knows how to navigate his boat through the peaks and valleys of the ocean tides towards new adventures.

Life before birth is a preparation for the first breath. Life after birth is learning the art of breathing to grow in love and consciousness. Life after death is disappearing into eternal breath. Breathing changes gradually throughout life. The waves of breathing carry us through our entire life, from the wild seas of our youth to the silent waters of old age.

Consciously surfing on the waves of breathing make us discover the intensity, the vitality, of each moment in our life. It gives us a perfect experience of living totally and joyfully in the eternal play of birth, death and rebirth.

19

Trusting life and going with its flow is the philosophy of natural breathing. When the in and out breath are in harmony we enjoy the orgasmic meeting of life and death in the experience of love.

The Soul of Healthy Breathing

The ancient Greeks localised the seat of the soul in the middle of our body around the height of the diaphragm. Even if we don't agree, at least we have to acknowledge that the diaphragm is the most important breath-supporting muscle complex. As such, it is the key to our breathing and it strongly influences all our important life-supporting processes.

The diaphragm reaches across the middle of our body, at the point where the chest and the belly meet. Being fixed on the lower part of the chest bone, the lower rib cage, the spine and close to the back and belly muscles, it separates the upper and the lower body. It is not only an organ for breathing but it also connects and integrates the two worlds around the belly and the chest – physiologically, psychologically and energetically.

The diaphragm works in the middle of our body - moving up with the exhalation and down with the inhalation. In a relaxed state, inhalation and exhalation are in good balance. By the smooth, rhythmical contraction and relaxation of the diaphragm and other related muscles, the breath moves like a gentle wave through our body and can give us an oceanic feeling of life.

There are many movements in nature, which remind me of the working of the diaphragm. Often I find myself gazing at large birds flying with ease high in the sky. I enjoy seeing trees waving in the wind or the play of a leaf carried away by a strong breeze.

Once, while I was scuba diving in the Mexican Caribbean, I was lucky to see a stingray – a big flat fish – gliding with its huge wings over the ocean floor. I was amazed at what a beautiful feeling its harmonious movements could trigger in my body merely by watching it! I realised this was the language of a relaxed diaphragm.

This same indescribable feeling of harmony, freedom, gracefulness and sensuality touches me in so many different ways in my work with breath therapy. In fact, it is the same feeling that I have touched many times during breathing sessions when I relaxed into a delightful and easy rhythm of breathing, feeling as if existence was carrying and caressing me.

Health and Rejuvenation through Inner Massage

One of the most forgotten miracles of our body is its ability to massage, cleanse and heal itself by natural breathing. Through the rising and falling movement of the diaphragm each breath massages all areas and organs of our body. Its massage eliminates waste material, supports the blood flow, relaxes tensions and keeps us open and energetic, thus allowing good blood circulation and oxygen saturation on the level of microcirculation in all body tissues.

In Chinese medicine it is known that body or organ tensions are often related to unresolved physical and psychological stress. It is interesting that in the diaphragm the physical and the psychological meet in a biological structure. It combines two different muscular systems. One we can consciously use to activate our breathing and release stress. The other works unconsciously and autonomously, which means that it breathes and releases stress without us even being aware of it.

Psychologically speaking, the diaphragm and our breathing are a meeting point of our conscious and unconscious. That is why the massage like movement of the diaphragm supports our physiological as much as our psychological wellbeing and prevents us from developing dis-ease.

In our chest, the movement of the breath wave caused by the diaphragm massages the lungs, the heart and also the thymus gland, which is important for the strengthening of our immune system. It is also vibrating into the neck, the head and the arms. That's why healthy breathing and a flexible body structure are essential especially for preventing heart and related vascular dis-ease. The wave of breathing reaches the heart from the outside, where its life-supporting vessels are located and keeps them open and young. This allows the blood to nourish and energise the heart muscle.

One important psychological risk factor for heart attack is often overlooked; it is hidden animosity. This means nothing other than blocked emotions, especially repressed anger. Blocking emotions is only possible by blocking the movement of our breathing. We contract our chest, tighten our belly and hold our breath. The wave of breathing can't unfold to give the heart and its vessels a deep cleansing massage. And with time they may close and threaten our life.

The effect of the diaphragm's breath massage on other organs is similar. For example, breath massage keeps the solar plexus, the sun centre of our nervous system, relaxed and "shining." We experience it as a feeling of physical and psychological warmth, which protects us from the dark night of depression. Imagine the solar plexus is like the inner sun of our inner body's universe. Whatever lives inside this universe is affected by its warm radiation!

In the belly the wave of breathing supports the digestive organs. Bowel movement supported by deep breathing is good for our digestion! That's why a little walk after a good meal can greatly help our digestion. Finally, our respiration reaches to the pelvis and massages, cleans and revitalises our reproductive organs. Therefore, obviously, correct breathing is essential for our sexual health.

The quality of this inner massage depends on the strength and rhythm of our breathing. The better we breathe, the deeper the massage will be and the better our health will be. In short, with each breath life is massaging us! With each breath life is touching, cleaning and rejuvenating our body. A good touch feels like love for the body and with each breath we can feel loved by existence. With each breath we can feel that we are part of this beautiful life.

The wave of breathing relaxes, energises and integrates the body, the mind, the heart and the spirit. Being aware of the central function of the diaphragm, we can say that the body's flexibility – its ability to react to stressful influences and to stay healthy – depends on the flexibility of the diaphragm. Working with the breath and the powerful diaphragm has a truly holistic healing and preventive health effect.

Being in Touch with Life

Receiving a massage is a great pleasure. There is hardly anybody who does not like it. It does on the outside of our body exactly what our breath does on the inside. In each moment of our life it gives us a good feeling with a wonderful relaxed and joyful view of life. It connects us in a loving way with ourselves. Theoretically we should be happy and enjoy the touch of our breathing. But why don't we dare to breathe deeply?

Being touched is very beautiful, but it can also sometimes provoke a lot of fear – the fear of intimacy. From the very beginning of our life, touch has been an expression of intimacy. In our mother's womb we were surrounded by the womb itself, which was moving in rhythm with her breathing and massaging us, with this rhythm of her breath we were connected to the rhythm of life.

Birth was a shock because the smooth touch of the womb suddenly changed to the tough pressure in the birth channel with painful birth contractions. We were pushed out and our screaming afterwards showed the degree of our disappointment.

We really needed a loving touch after this painful experience; and if we did not receive it, throughout our whole life we may have suffered from an inability to relax deeply. Whenever somebody touches us today it might remind us of the pain related to missing this early touch and we are even afraid of being touched.

One of the most healing and supportive things a mother can do is to massage her baby regularly. It is a fantastic way to share her love and compassion and will allow the child to develop its physical, emotional and social intelligence. It will teach the baby the basic lessons of intimacy; love for the body, trust in the human being and compassion with life. It will make the baby take a deep breath into life.

Lovers can travel on the same road in order to come close and to maintain an intimate and loving relationship through sharing a loving touch. So often I meet people in my work that complain of not having being touched by their partners for years. Without being able to touch each other in their present life, they often feel a growing distance with each other.

A loving touch can create miracles and can bring a fresh breath into our relationships. It can even save the lives of those amongst us, who are "out of touch with life" and are longing for a sign of love in their empty world.

The Diaphragm Meditation

We have the idea that we are superior to animals. But in many ways we can learn from them. Researching their natural healing reflexes can help us to remember forgotten ways of curing ourselves. For example, when a dog is tense, afraid or out of breath, his whole body pants. You can see the work of his diaphragm moving in his belly and chest without restriction and releasing his tension.

Young and innocent children still carry this quality of spontaneous stress release. They scream, cry, laugh, sing or playfully imitate animals; the movement of their diaphragm in these activities keeps their breathing open. They don't keep their emotions stuck and enclosed in tense bellies or closed chests. That's why their bellies are so soft and relaxed and why they have such an enormous energy, an energy many adults can only dream of.

This reminds me of the Zen tradition, where masters give their disciples the exercise to dissolve simple and paradoxical messages about spiritual life to help their inner liberation. These messages have only one purpose: to stop the compulsively thinking mind, to become silent and one with oceanic consciousness.

Once, a disciple asked his master about the meaning of life. The master went down on his hands and knees and began panting like a dog. This was his way to answer the question; the meaning of life is breathing and living naturally like the animals. Live in the here and now – totally – and you become conscious.

Now let's take this technique into a little meditation to release the tension of our diaphragm, vitalise our body and refresh our spirits to master our breathing. We can do the meditation standing, sitting or lying down.

Stage 1: 5 Minutes Alternating Breathing

Here you play with alternating breathing. For five minutes keep on taking one breath into the belly and the next one into the chest. Play with your diaphragm moving the two big breathing spaces of belly and chest to move all the muscles in this area. This might wake up feelings related to contractions in the diaphragm, which you can release in the next stage.

Stage 2: 5 Minutes Shaking the Diaphragm

Now learn to distress your diaphragm by vibrating it. With your mouth open, shake up your diaphragm by short, rapid exhalations and inhalations. Let the rhythm of the breathing become a bit chaotic and let the whole body move with this chaos in your breathing. Then poke your tongue out a little and pant like a dog; this will release more tensions in the diaphragm.

Stage 3: 5 Minutes Feeling the Movement of the Breathing

Then relax your breathing. Place your hands on the lower ribcage and feel the soft movement of each breath. Visualise the big diaphragm working below your hands horizontally to the axis of your body. Imagine it moves harmoniously up and down like the wings of an eagle flying high in the sky.

It massages, cleans and rejuvenates your whole body. It also touches your solar plexus bringing warmth and light into your body, releasing feelings of depression and gently connecting the breathing of the belly and the chest.

Stage 4: 5 Minutes Relaxing

Sit or lie down for five minutes. Enjoy the relaxation, freshness and delight in your whole body. Allow the breathing to float freely and harmoniously.

Chapter 4

Breathing with Pleasure

*The moment you breathe deeply, sex energy is released; it
has to be released. It has to flow all over your being. Then your
body will become orgasmic.*

Osho

Giving a Fresh Breath to Our Relationships

Why is breathing so important for our relationships? What
has it to do with intimacy? These are questions, which
hardly anyone ever asks because the power of correct
breathing is widely forgotten, not only in life, but also in
the meeting together of a man and a woman.

Learning to breathe with pleasure is a way of healing and
enjoying ourselves in intimate relationships. In my working
with people, I have come to realise that many individuals
miss a deep energetic understanding of themselves. They
also miss understanding the intimacy of their relating due to
their superficial breathing.

We learn to use breathing for control instead of for
enjoying ourselves and so we cause immense frustration in
our relationships, controlling each other rather than
enjoying each other. We miss the great treasures of
intimacy because we don't dare breathe wholeheartedly, to
enjoy our body, to enjoy sex and orgasm together.

To experience pleasure, first we need to love and to accept
ourselves; this means most of all to know and understand

29

the mysteries of our body. Then enjoying the other will have a foundation in our self and can give a new fragrance to our relationships. Also, sharing our pleasure in an open space with a friend can bring gratefulness and a loving understanding of the other sex.

Bringing awareness to our breathing and feeling the juice of life each breath brings, will allow us to experience the great pleasure of living in the body, our very own body. When breathing with pleasure we can feel our sexual life energy and will learn to trust and relax into it. This energy helps us to enjoy the strong breathing related to sexual activity as much as the soft breathing when opening our heart to love.

Accepting the basic longing of our body to feel pleasure, we have a foundation to rise towards the "higher pleasures" of life by refining our energies, passing through the different stages of our life from passion to compassion.

Sex or Suicide

Our education does not teach us to develop our breath, thus enabling us to rejoice in the pleasures of life. Instead of enjoying life, we learn to control and repress it. Our sexuality is loaded with guilt, comparison, feelings of inferiority and the fear of intimacy. We dream of sex but we don't actually live it the way we long for. We suffer from an unfulfilled sex life leading to anger and frustration.

But as anger is also judged, we move to the next stage of repression - trying to repress our sex and our anger, compensating for them by continual greed. We consume everything and anything to feel some secondary sense of fulfilment. A feeling of emptiness remains and soon greed leads to boredom with life, depression and ultimately to suicide. Sex energy repressed ultimately has the potential to kill us.

The last thing S. remembered was being transported to a hospital. She was broken-hearted, feeling guilty about the suicide of her father when she was sixteen and also about her twenty-three-year old son, who had just recently committed suicide by hanging himself.

Trying some different conventional therapies and failing to get back her joy for life, everything in chaos, she finally gave up and she herself decided to commit suicide. Luckily she was saved at the last minute.

I met her six months later, when she had recovered some longing to live and was reconnecting with her energy. We worked on unlocking her energy by mobilising her pelvis, related to the natural movement of deep breathing. Passing through many emotional expressions she finally remembered the days of her early teenage years.

She was playing sexually with a much older man, who was known to lack in morality. Years later it became known that this man had played with other children and people had felt that he was guilty of abusing them. She became confused because she felt that somehow she had enjoyed the meetings with him. However, she felt deeply confused about this situation and was not able to share it. As a result she cut off from her sexual energy and got stuck in a strong feeling of guilt, projecting it on all aspects in her life.

In the process of her therapeutic work she realised that an adult is responsible for his or her own life and that the suicide of her father and that of her adult son were not her responsibility. Yes, she may have made many mistakes, but problems or situations can be resolved in a different manner – such as receiving therapy rather than attempting suicide. Instead of hating and torturing herself through guilt as she had done for years, she was very angry about what they had done; ruining her life through the guilt they had engendered.

She became furious in an energetic breathing session, all her frustrations were released and suddenly her prematurely aged-looking face was transformed. She became a young woman, suddenly enjoying her vibrant energy again. Shortly after, she started relating with younger men, enjoying her body and feeling sexual again. After she had allowed her long-repressed rage out, the guilt was gone and she could also see the sexual experience of her teens with new eyes.

Reconnecting to Our Life Energy

Yes, sleeping and hidden beyond depression, greed, anger and suicidal tendencies, is our very life energy, our sexual energy. Sexual energy needs a dynamic and transformative therapy such as *Osho Diamond Breath* and active meditation to enable emotional expression to release the blocks surrounding the energy. We can then return to the fire of our original energy, the energy that we brought into this life being an innocent wild and spontaneous child. It is the beginning of our inner flowering into love, freedom and creativity.

We have learnt to behave, following the social rules and respecting the laws, which are required to organise a society. We have not learnt that these regulations are simply mental tools developed to run life and protect us, but they are not life itself. We use them if they are needed, but otherwise we need to be able to live the deeper dimensions of life; the pleasure of our body, the joy of our heart and the art of being.

The problem is, we stay identified with all these regulations even when they are not needed. They have become our life and made it mechanical and lifeless! We have forgotten the real life, which is present in the aliveness of a young child or the love and peacefulness of a living Buddha.

In fact, we are attracted to a spontaneous child or a living Buddha and long for the freedom they experience, but at the same time we are afraid to break the rules and lose our old sense of security. We are afraid to lose the only security we think we have – the security of our mind – and therefore go crazy.

We are afraid to end up in chaos and to a certain extent we are right. If rules are broken unconsciously, the damn of social behaviour breaks. Old repressions surface and unload in orgies of violence, like in war, pornography and crime. All negativity is released; the negativity that is caused by living and feeling, as though in a prison of rules and which is kept in control by the same rules. Instead of bringing awareness to this situation and releasing these tensions consciously, in meditative therapy, we create a new law to keep them even more repressed.

We have forgotten that below this layer of negativity lies the layer of our positive life energy – the layer of our free pulsing and innocent life energy. It is like drilling for oil: we drill through many unpleasant layers of earth until we find the fluid gold in the depth of mother earth. In order to reach to our inner layer of gold, we need to take the courage to question all our beliefs and drop life-negative attitudes. We need to learn to pass consciously through a healing chaos in order to reach the treasures of our inner world.

The Pelvis Breathing Meditation

Going for a joyful walk is one of the greatest pleasures in life. Strolling along, while we sense and breathe in the fragrance of the fresh forest air, stretching out on the ground and moving our spine, or singing playfully are all wonderful experiences. Why is it so?

One of the main reasons for the pleasure we feel from such experiences is that during them we get a taste of our pelvis moving in rhythm with our breathing, with the rhythm of nature. When our body relaxes and our pelvis swings freely forward and backward with each breath, living is a joy. Life becomes a dance, which in turn awakens our senses and opens our heart. We feel in tune with nature.

A very negative result of our education is learning to control our feelings by controlling our breathing and its movements in our body. We need to understand that a key to open for deeper breathing is to move and allow the pelvis to swing. If we stop this movement, our pelvis becomes like a dead rock losing its ability to give us feelings of pleasure. A little meditation can help us to learn, to play with the swinging of our pelvis in rhythm with our breathing to enjoy ourselves.

Deep breathing can give us an experience of the opening of the body's energy flow - from the pelvis to the chest. Let's remember that being sexual and attractive is a question of our energy and our inner quality, rather than our outer appearance. Let's remember, also, that our pelvis is the foundation of our body and our breathing and the location of our sex centre.

Stage 1: 5 Minutes Spontaneous Body Stretching

Begin with moving around and stretching your body in a manner that you will start to feel more open, natural and flexible. If you notice some physical contractions take some time to tune into them and gently stretch them out. Wherever there is pain, that's where your energy is stuck. It wants to move and flow again, so help your energy as much as you can by creating your own forms of stretching.

As an old Tantric saying goes: "Become like a cat." Allow spontaneous movements to support the need of your body to feel free. If you have learned the discipline of Yoga, put it aside for a moment and try this playful approach to open your body-mind, heart and soul. Let control go and be open for some unpredictable and surprising movements in your body.

Stage 2: 5 Minutes Slowly Opening and Closing Your Legs

In the second stage, lie down on your back on a blanket or mattress. Bring your knees up and let the soles of your feet remain together and flat on the floor. Now let the legs slowly open and then slowly close while your breathing follows the needs of your body. If your legs start shaking spontaneously just allow it.

Feel the opening of your pelvic floor. The opening and closing of your legs moves many muscles connected to your pelvis and releases their tensions. You might come in contact with feelings of vulnerability and sensitivity related to your sex.

Stage 3: 5 Minutes Gentle Pelvis Breathing

Remaining on the blanket, keep your knees up and open your legs with the soles of your feet on the ground shoulder width apart. Your arms should be a little open also and the whole body relaxed. Breathe a little deeper through your open mouth and feel the exhalation and inhalation. Then start rolling the pelvis gently, in rhythm with your breathing. With the inhalation it moves backwards and down into the floor. With the exhalation it moves forwards and up towards the ceiling.

Allow the movement to come from your legs instead of your belly - a very gentle, sensitive movement and one that is connected to your breathing. If you stay relaxed you can feel how the body likes to follow the movement of the pelvis. Let the soft movement of your breathing become like a wave in your body, moving from the belly to the chest and back to the belly. Allow the wave of breathing to touch your innermost being and to refresh your spirits.

Stage 4: 5 Minutes Relaxing

Slowly relax. Come to rest, allowing your body to stretch out on the floor. Feel yourself open and energised by this gentle experience of pelvic breathing. Watch the breath touching your body.

Chapter 5

Breathing in Tantra

All meditation is essentially the experience of sex without sex.

Osho

The Joy of Tantric Breathing

In Tantra we learn about a beautiful way to liberate our life energy and support our transformation from the world of sex to the world of love and meditation. As I mentioned before, many people miss the energetic understanding of themselves and their intimate relationships because of their superficial breathing. If we incorrectly learn to use breath to control, instead of enjoying ourselves, we cause ourselves to be terribly frustrated and miss the treasures of intimacy. Worse, we can even become afraid of it.

Tantra accepts life in its totality. It reconnects us to the energetic roots in our sexual body and leads us towards the inner core of our being. Once we can enjoy ourselves with all that nature has given to us, soon the wings of love will open and we will remember ourselves as a free spirit breathing and celebrating life.

It seems too good to be true what our breath can do: releasing tensions, discovering our forgotten energies, enjoying the richness of life through our body, or experiencing a new dimension of spiritual being. Just by feeling good with ourselves we begin loving ourselves in such a profound way, a way we have never done before.

Without roots in our sexual body, we live like a cut flower, weak, dependent, with a short lifetime and without the ability to grow strong, creative and independent. We miss the possibility of our life energy rising to the peaks of fulfilment and joy. We are like lame ducks without the energy to fly into the open sky of enlightenment.

To keep a human being weak, all we need to do is to repress the sexual energy and make it the enemy of his very own body, hiding and hating it. He will start feeling guilty about his sex and judge his own body and lose all self-trust and self-love. We deprive him of his roots and his energy.

This human being will become like a Japanese Bonsai tree. Whenever it grows stronger roots, they are cut so that it will stay forever small. It totally forgets its potential to grow high and powerful and to give birth to thousands of beautiful blossoms. It is cute to look at, but it lives an impotent life because it was never allowed to grow up.

Tantric Healing and the River of Love

A river is nourished by water falling from mountain springs into wild waterfalls and then, through the many creeks streaming into it. Similarly, our capacity to love and grow in spirit depends on our sexual energy being nourished and refined in the course of life by the experiences of birth, childhood, puberty and adulthood. The more we accept our sexual energy, the greater is our potential to rise in love and lightness.

Because of our conditioning, through physical, emotional and mental tensions, we have not only blocked the spring of our sexual energy and the flow but also stopped the river of love. As a result repressed fear, anger, sadness or even happiness keeps us stuck and often we feel heavy like a rock. With deep breathing and Tantric meditations, we can melt these rocks and empower our health, sexual energy and capacity to love.

Some time ago an attractive young man came to our workshop. He shared with all present that everything in his life was perfect; he was perfect. In fact everything was too perfect and he simply could not feel anything. He had been with many women before his marriage and now had a child. He loved his family but could not connect with them deeply. He was worried that his son would become like him and that's why he attended the workshop.

His body was totally tight. He tried to be the best in everything and to constantly have our attention. At one point we began *Tantric Breathing* by moving the pelvis connected to the rhythm of breathing. He began to experience a lot of pain in his lower back and belly and started to feel and remember the ongoing pressure his parents placed on him by their expectations. In fact he was the favourite of his mother – "mother's little helper" – especially around the time his parents separated, when he was 9-years-old.

While working with another member of the group on a problem related to incest, he became aware of his sexual attraction, as a boy, to his mother. He remembered the way she seduced him, but at the same time rejected him unconsciously. He could see again how she kept him away from his father and also put him in a situation of competing with his father. This is the same competition that he felt to this very day that he has with men.

In the next breathing session he suddenly started feeling how disconnected he had been to his pelvis. He was heartbroken about all the women he had used for sex without having really connected with them because he could not even connect to himself. That was the day when he dropped his dead perfection and stopped breathing like a machine. His sex and his heart started to connect and he became the sensitive, vulnerable boy he once had been.

Tantra – The Rediscovery of Spontaneity

The rediscovery of Tantra in modern days has led to a lot of confusion. *Tantric Healing* is not about sexual indulgence, nor is it about denying it. They are two sides of the same coin. They are extremes caused by a mind conditioned by sexual repression.

A typical example is when some well-respected man publicly condemns sexual indulgence until, finally, a newspaper discovers his secret addictions and perversions. Then the habitual feeling of guilt occurs; he excuses himself but soon he is caught again. Why is it so difficult to accept and enjoy our human nature and our needs as sexual beings without hiding and becoming slaves to the perversions of our mind?

In ancient Tantra schools, the adept was only accepted if he had a relaxed and conscious relationship with his sex life and was not a slave to his sexual desires, thus being able to ride on the waves of sexual energy towards the ultimate orgasm of meditation. Reading Osho's *Vigyan Bhairav Tantra* gives us a unique sense of how meditation based on the acceptance of sexual energy can open ourselves for bliss and ecstasy.

We easily get confused when people try to bring techniques from old Tantra scriptures made for people in former centuries into modern life. All these ancient techniques were made for a very different lifestyle. At that time it was easy for people, because their life consisted of strong physical work with little mental input. For modern man, the situation is completely the opposite with little physical work and a lot of mental input. He therefore needs a new and contemporary approach.

Today's life is so organised with all kinds of mental disciplines that we need to rediscover a spontaneous approach in order to liberate our life energy instead of adding more discipline. In this sense, the popular practice of Yoga is not very helpful as it only strengthens our already too-disciplined mind. We need an approach that makes us less, instead of more, controlled. We need a Tantric approach to life.

Once I had a client coming for individual therapy complaining about painful tensions in his lower belly. After some chitchatting he told me proudly that he could give women many orgasms because he practices an old Eastern technique of holding his ejaculation back in sex. His ego was happy but his body was extremely tense. The simple advice to relax into spontaneous orgasm healed his pain.

People, who are relaxed and joyful in their bodies can do these techniques, otherwise they lead to more contraction. Today the first thing to learn is how to actively release the enormous tensions we have, especially if we desire to use these techniques. This is the unique insight of active meditation and Osho's contemporary approach to Tantra.

This is not about repeating old rituals, but about learning to trust the spontaneous flow of life's energy without getting caught up in our fears. We can then relax, breathe, feel and become sensitive and sensual again, instead of focusing on better sexual techniques. We liberate our love life from the mechanical behaviour caused by our tense mind. We learn to enjoy sex as a beautiful play in the process of growing up.

Overcoming Schizophrenia

Concerning our body, we live in a state of schizophrenia. As mentioned before, our shallow breathing is the result of blocking our principle breathing muscle, the diaphragm, which is a horizontal structure in the middle of our body. It splits our body into a "public" upper and a "private" lower part. We separate sex from the heart and we separate our roots in sex from the wings of love.

As we are also afraid of our emotions, we contract our belly so that there is no space for the breath to expand. Being afraid to be vulnerable and to open our heart, we also contract our chest. Now we sit in the trap of our own tense body and there is not much space for breathing left. We breathe enough to survive but not enough to enjoy life. We accumulate a minimum of life energy, but we fall short of the experience that the overflow of life energy provided by the teachings of Tantra can give us.

It appears that we are hiding in our contracted body like a warrior in his castle. Cut off from our roots and not enjoying our body, we feel as though we are "hanging in the air", insecure and powerless! We have lost our "grounding" in life and all that is left now for us to do is to compensate our insecurity by moving our energy into the head and thinking about life instead of living it.

In fact, we are confused! We can hide and repress our sex energy but our body doesn't forget it. The energy has to go somewhere. If it cannot flow freely it gets stuck in muscular and organic tension throughout the body, making us feel heavy, depressed and chronically tired. It gives us everything from lower back pain to a headache. We attack and suffocate ourselves with our inner pressure. Energy, repressed and displaced, becomes destructive.

How do we correct and put order into our body, our original temple, to celebrate life? We need to rediscover our body and our breathing because these are the keys to a rich life!

Breathing has to become the golden wind to cleanse our body, mind, heart and spirit from old tensions, repressions, perversions and schizophrenias! Only then we can walk along the path of Tantra and find our way from the sexual orgasm of the body to the ultimate orgasm of consciousness.

The Flame of Life Meditation

Our sexual energy – life energy – has been twisted by many moralistic beliefs. It has been programmed into what we call sexuality today. If we can liberate our sexual energy from these old repressions, the energy will be able to move back to where it belongs; from the pornographic ideas in the head to an energetic experience of our sex centre. The flame of life energy can burn in the correct place again, warming and transforming our life.

From compressing sex and overheating our body-mind and causing conflict in our love life, the same energy can also lift us, relax us and liberate us by flowing freely. The fire of passion burning in our sex centre can move us through the agonies and the ecstasies, the dramas and the comedies of relationship, towards the delight and enjoyment of a compassionate heart.

A sexually relaxed body is warm and healthy; a doctor knows this when he can feel our warm hands and feet. A warm pelvis is a healthy pelvis. It is free of contraction and has a good blood circulation. It provides the body with a solid energetic foundation and sexual energy works like a "central heating" for our whole body. We look relaxed, warm and with a healthy taint. We need neither make-up nor lipstick as a good blood circulation gives us the most natural appearance.

In fact, if we feel cold or tense, it is best to sit on a warm place to relax and warm up our pelvis. Soon the whole body will be warm again. Guess why cats like to rest on a warm stove!

The following meditation helps us to reconnect and warm up our pelvis, relax our genitals and open our pelvic floor. We can feel this warm life energy expanding into our whole body and making us feel at home within ourselves. It is like sitting on mother earth and being warmed up by the tremendous fire burning deep in the core of our planet.

Stage 1: 5 Minutes Opening the Pelvis

Gently begin to dance to some soft music that you like. This will help vitalise your breathing and it will be energising. While dancing find some ways to play with your pelvis, moving and stretching it. Bend your knees a little more and open your pelvic floor by moving it down towards the earth.

Feel your whole body warming up, especially your legs and your pelvis. In reflexology, around your heels are the foot reflex zones of your pelvis and sexual organs; you might like to involve them more in your movements. Also open your mouth a little to breathe deeper, thus supporting the opening of your sex.

Stage 2: 5 Minutes Sitting on Fire

Now sit down, keep your body straight and close your eyes. Feel your body and your pelvis and start contracting your pelvic floor for a moment. Then rub your hands until they are hot and put one hand under your pelvic floor between your legs. Feel the warmth of your hand warming up the pelvic floor; relax and breathe gently into it.

Imagine you are sitting on fire. Red, orange and yellow flames flicker in your pelvis and fill it with warmth. Allow the body to breathe and softly move with the flames rising up in the body, melting its contractions and slowly radiating into all of your body.

Stage 3: 5 Minutes Becoming the Flame of Life

Slowly stand up and imagine that you become the flame of life. Let yourself move like a flame in the wind. Enjoy your soft life energy. Imagine its warmth rising up in the body, keeping you alive, healthy and young. Rejoice in being sexual and sensual in your whole body.

Stage 4: 5 Minutes Relaxing

Now sit or lie down, relax and enjoy your warm soft body. Watch your gentle breathing and feel the juice of life pulsing inside.

Chapter 6

Breathing and Relaxing the Mind

Mind and breath are so much connected, have to be,
because breathing is life. A man can be without mind, but
cannot be without breathing. Breathing is deeper than mind.
If you change breathing, you change thinking.

Osho

The Mind is the Problem!

For everything that goes wrong in our life we have a
tendency to blame; we blame somebody else or we blame
ourselves. By changing our outer circumstances or by
changing our behaviour, we think our situation in the future
will improve and be better   Wrong, the Buddha would say;
it's the mind that causes us to be in permanent conflict with
this beautiful life and unaware of our inner blissfulness.

A pessimistic and depressive view of life is the result of a
long process of mental intoxication, starting early in our
childhood. From the first days of our life, our innocent
mind is fed with often life-negative beliefs from people
around us who don't realise what they are doing to us. They
put their ideas into us before we can even experience life
and ask our own questions and find our own answers.

As a result, these ideas will haunt us throughout our life
and prevent us from moving in the natural flow of our own
life. Following their ideas, we live their life and naturally
repeat the same mistakes, which have made their life
unhappy.

49

You should control your feelings! You should not show your feelings and should be polite! You should do this and you should not do that – a whole catechism of beliefs are hammered into our being without giving us the opportunity initially to ask the questions we have about life and ourselves.

"What's your name?" asks the teacher to the newly arrived scholars in the classroom. A small boy in the back raises his hands and answers, "My name is Don't!" "Don't?" asks the teacher. "Yes, my father always says 'don't' to me! 'Don't do this and don't do that!'"

The mind can be helpful, but it can also be dangerous. In science, for instance, the mind can be used well to secure our survival and to create a comfortable materialistic world. If we know how to relax the mind and if we are able to take time out from it and have periods of silence, it is really a fantastic instrument. But unfortunately the majority of us cannot do this; therefore, the mind becomes a dictator, keeping us compulsively thinking, stressed, sleepless and nervous. We cannot stop it.

Asking the Heart for Support

Western life style is synonymous with having sleep problems. Even in the night the mind doesn't give us the urgently needed rest! We cannot fall asleep because the events of the day still haunt us. We wake up in the middle of the night and the mind keeps us so busy that we cannot fall asleep again. Or, we wake up early in the morning full of fear and worry. It is no accident that many heart attacks happen in the early hours of the morning.

A good night's rest is over even before it begins. A good night of rejuvenating breath is disturbed and our "batteries" cannot be recharged. A restful night relaxing into our belly breathing is not possible and this keeps us tense and tired. We don't get what we urgently need in our modern stressful environment; a moment of inner silence and peacefulness.

Unless we learn how to relax the mind through meditation, we will not be able to escape the endless mental activity. The more we are lost in thinking, the more tense we become and the further adrift in the sea of madness. The mind becomes a hellish machine. The joy of temporary mind activity becomes the agony of compulsive thinking. Even in sex we keep on thinking, become busy with pornographic fantasies and thus miss the height of orgasm; a moment of not thinking.

Being stuck in the mind, we cannot feel much. We are lonely and separated and easily lose the awareness of all those aspects of life that make it so beautiful; moving with a spontaneous flow, relaxing, trusting, loving and simply enjoying the art of being.

The moment the mind cools down, then the heart - our feeling centre - begins to open and vibrate and we feel connected and in harmony with the inner and the outer world. We experience a wholeness, which we long for so much.

For the mind to relax, we need to learn to ask our heart for support. The moment we acknowledge the heart and listen to its language of feeling and presence, it is ready to change our life for the better. Yes, we have forgotten the heart for a long time, but it is patiently waiting for us and it will be immensely grateful and ready to guide our ship from the madness of a dictatorial mind towards the safe haven of love and inner freedom.

From a Dead Serious Relationship

Our relationships are a mirror of our mind. The more dependent we are on the mind and the less we feel at home in our heart, the more dependent and less loving we will be with our partners. The more expectations we carry in our mind, the more expectations we have on our partners and these are prone to cause problems.

The mind judges, hopes, believes, compares, competes, pushes, manipulates or dreams. It makes us feel guilty, jealous, inferior and restless or freaked out and becomes desperate if life develops differently than it expected.

The ideas of our mind are like a covering of dust, which prevent us from having a clear view of reality. These ideas give us either a positive self-image – that we are the greatest star on earth, or a negative self-image in which we see ourselves as the greatest failure the world has ever seen. The mind pretends to know everything, but at the same time it keeps us in a permanent conflict with reality.

The crux of the problem is that we have learned to believe only in the mind, to take our mind serious but not our feelings. By making ourselves totally dependent on the mind, we get trapped in its dream world and become insane because we lose contact with the real world around and inside of us. We can neither value the mind's qualities nor see its deficiencies. We lose all objectivity.

It is like being in a bad relationship where we are blindly addicted to each other. We neither can relax, nor love each other, nor can we separate. As I mentioned before, the only way out of this harmful relationship is to learn to relax and to learn to see the mind from a perspective of loving awareness. What does this mean?

To live a fulfilled life we need to learn to enjoy all its different dimensions, the intelligence of the body, the mind, the heart and the being. Then the mind becomes just one small player in our life, which we can carefully watch and stop if it oversteps its responsibilities. It cannot anymore overpower all other areas of our intelligence and we can rejoice in a natural connection with life again.

We have forgotten that we were born free of thinking and fully connected to the breath of life. We have forgotten that those moments, when we were part of life without any interpretation by the mind, were the most innocent, joyful and mysterious moments of our life.

Out of the fear of not being able to survive as children, we have developed a mind that wants to please others so that they love us and don't harm us. We have learnt to trust others more than ourselves and make our sense of self-worthiness dependent on their approval.

Today, if others love us, we feel happy. If they don't love us, we feel unhappy and fight for their acknowledgement. Or we reject them before they can reject us. If we are as successful as they wish us to be, we feel great. If we don't live up to their expectations, we feel desperate. We miss being integrated individuals following our own truth and being in harmony with ourselves.

To a Joyful Relationship

Yes, we were made to be afraid of breathing into our own life and now we need to find our own breath again. We have lost the contact to our inner being, which naturally vibrates love, self-respect and dignity, independent from the opinion of others. Constant mind activity has hindered us from remembering our inner breath. Our inner growth is now to search for this diamond inside ourselves, to unearth it and to make it shine again.

Joyful relationships have a simple recipe: learn to breathe deeply, let go of the mind, enjoy the body and open the heart! The most beautiful moments happen when we have no judgments, when we are relaxed and feel a loving presence with the other. It's like falling in love and we don't judge and we don't care if people judge us. We are "madly" in love and might do outrageous things, which we are usually afraid of because they could ruin our reputation as serious people.

Once being hopelessly in love, I entered the office of my beloved. Full of excitement I started rolling over the floor like a child until I reached her desk and jumped into her arms. You should have seen the faces of her co-workers, their judgments written on their faces. However, the beautiful shy smile on her face was enough for me to feel blessed by an existence that permitted me to find this wonderful woman.

The problem in our relationships is that soon after an overwhelming honeymoon, the mind storms back to claim its dictatorship. For a moment we did not think too much, but now it starts again. We start thinking and planning our life with the other, build up securities to protect our love, begin to claim the other as "my beloved" and marry to give birth to "our children". We are falling back into the trap of the possessive mind, dominating our sexuality and our heart.

For a brief moment we felt this beautiful glimpse of love and now we start losing it again. We felt so free, so open and so connected to life and all our friends and now we start blaming each other: "You don't really love me! You don't really care for me!" The mind possesses us again and we want to possess our partner. The mind changes us again and we want to change our partner. We start fighting and don't understand why all the beauty we shared together is disappearing. The mind is the boss again.

Relationships can only work if we meditate together to relax the mind and open our hearts. The partner mirrors our state of being. In our relationships we can cause constant problems and keep our minds busy by solving them. Or we can learn together to drop the mind, enjoy our bodies, share a loving hug and relax into a space of silent understanding from the heart.

The Power of Breathing to Relax the Mind

In changing the breath we can change our life. Breath is the hidden bridge between all dimensions of our being. It interconnects all areas of our life. If we hold our breath by a tense, fearful, angry or worried mind, it causes tension in the body and pressure on the heart, while it suffocates the soul.

It is an open secret that the breath reflects and influences our state of mind. Relaxed breathing creates a relaxed mind. A Buddha's breathing is calm and effortless and so is his mind. To reach a calm state of mind we need to reach a calm state of breathing - neither repressive nor expressive.

There are two ways to achieve this: directly or indirectly. We can immediately start and try to breathe calmly and deeply. But with the amount of stress we usually carry this is pretty difficult. Or, we can breathe wildly and release our tensions and then we will naturally relax into deep, calm breathing afterwards.

However, exhalation is the key to letting go of stress and finding inner balance. Automatically, the release of tension will enhance our inhalation too. Depending on our state of tenseness, the exhalation needs to be modulated between a simple, deep sigh or a forced, dynamic exhalation accompanied by some sound and emotional expression through intense body movement.

Consciously exhaling immediately releases tensions in the nervous system and relaxes us. Such a release gives us the distance we need in order to see ourselves better and to take ourselves a little less seriously. It makes it easier to watch our thought process rather than becoming hooked by it. Then our socially conditioned mind slowly loses control over our life and we become more ourselves living from the core of our inner being.

Rooted inside ourselves we lose the fear of being rejected for being the way we are. With a deep breath we can liberate blocked energy resources, which can now stream back into our life. We lost our breath by getting lost in the world of the mind. Now it's time to regain our unique quality of breath, allowing us to discover an eternally young spirit pulsing inside us.

It's time to live our passion for life and compassion for all living beings. It's time to transform our relationships from negativity, conflict and protectiveness to openness, acceptance and life affirmation. It's time to take a deep breath into the art of living – alone or together.

The Gibberish Meditation

High levels of stress cause high levels of mental activity; and high mental activity causes more stress and makes relaxation impossible. Ultimately it makes us feel sick and ruins our health. To relax, first we need to release a mountain of physical, emotional and mental tension. Once it is released, our breathing balances and we can see the mind for what it is – a faculty of constant dream creation.

When we stop automatically believing what the mind tells us, we can witness our thoughts without taking them on board! Losing our identification with the mind it loses its power and it cannot dominate or undermine our life and love affairs anymore. We can relax and become silent and peaceful.

In the late eighties, Osho invented a new active meditation to release mental tensions and called it "No Mind Meditation". He recommends this meditation in a shortened form for individuals with nervousness or sleeping problems. It's a beautiful method to empty the body-mind from the stresses of the day and to go to sleep in a relaxed condition. Nothing is more rejuvenating than to take a deep breath and to recharge our energies during a good night's sleep.

I love this meditation because it helps me to see with some inner distance how much madness the mind carries, to play with it and then to drop it. How can we take our mind serious if we see how crazy it can be? How can we take ourselves so serious if we see how blindly we have followed the madness of our mind? In fact, we learn not to take ourselves so seriously anymore because we learn not to take our mind so seriously anymore.

Just recently I met a participant of a former workshop at a beach restaurant in Tulum, Mexico and he told me: "You know what! Since you gave me this meditation three months ago, I am doing it every day. I sleep much better and my skin has become much better too!" For years he had suffered from sleeplessness, psoriasis and multiple sclerosis and all of his symptoms had decreased significantly.

Now let's do this meditation to come to our senses by talking non-sense.

Stage 1: 10 Minutes Talking Non-Sense

You can play with this meditation alone or with friends. Do it in a standing or sitting position. At night you can do it in your bed so that after the active part you can lie down and relax into a deep sleep.

Start talking nonsense in a language you don't know. If the surrounding allows, talk loudly and let all kind of sounds come with the nonsense words. If you have to do it silently because of other people being around, release your tensions by talking wildly without sound.

Express your emotions with the sound of your voice too.

Support it by breathing and moving the body – your face, head, shoulders, arms, pelvis and legs. Making strong grimaces helps you to really feel an effective physical, emotional and mental release of tension.

Stage 2: 10 Minutes Watching and Relaxing

Sit or lie down comfortably and close your eyes. Now relax and internally watch yourself silently, without judging anything. Observe what is happening in your body and your mind, in your heart and your soul. Relax into the eternal rhythm of your breathing.

Chapter 7

Breathing to Master Emotions

If you can become master of your breathing you become master of your emotions.

Osho

Overwhelming Emotions

Wow, I was so angry one day! It drove me crazy that my best friend had broken an agreement we had with each other concerning the protection of our work. Overwhelmed by my rage, I was looking for an outlet for this energy, but could not find anything. Just as well because it gave me time to cool down and relax again.

One day I crashed a car but survived without a scratch. Getting out of the car I was in shock. A driver watching my accident stopped and stepped out of his car to help me. Overwhelmed by the energy of fear, I needed a release. I was sure that this person had caused me to crash and I burst out with fury, blaming this poor guy for my accident. Just in time I became aware of my unconscious attack before causing more trouble for myself.

Another time on a flight from Cancun to Mexico City, I felt so beautifully relaxed and full of the joys of the Caribbean Sea. Looking out of the window I could see the famous volcano Popocatepetl coming closer. I was thinking what a wonderful majestic view when suddenly air turbulence heavily shook the plane. Taken by fear, I broke out in a cold sweat and was close to a panic attack. Just in time the shaking stopped and I could relax again. A little tequila did the rest to cool me down.

It was one of the happiest days in my life; after seven years of studying, I successfully finished my medical examination. Relieved from all the pressure of the past years, I was ready to run through the streets and scream my happiness out into the world. Luckily, some friends kept me grounded and saved me from some kind of embarrassment.

The tears did not seem to stop; for three days I had been crying because I realised that our relationship was finished. I felt such a deep romantic connection with my beloved, that I could not imagine being happy again without her. In total desperation, I left her. Soon after, in the middle of an icy winter day, I was gliding with my car into a ditch. Finally, getting my energy together and calling a truck to pull the car out of the ditch brought me back to reality. Some days later, I fell in love again with somebody else.

These are examples of what strong unconscious emotions can do. We lose control completely of ourselves; we are out of ourselves. Not surprising, because our emotions have been judged so many times that we did not learn to deal with them consciously. We feel like crying but our mind tells us that a man should not cry. We are split, knowing one thing but feeling something else. Finally, under pressure, we forget it all and have an unconscious emotional explosion

The Hidden Rulers of Our Life

Our unconscious emotions are the hidden rulers of our life! Originally they were helping us to protect ourselves and create a safe environment for expressing and fulfilling our needs. They are a simple instinctive, non-verbal language to communicate. We get afraid, angry, sad or happy in relationship to the outside world.

Like our mind, our emotions are orientated outwards. They need the other; they need a projection screen on the outside world to get working. But they cannot lead us towards our inner being. They are part of our body-mind.

Animals have the most primitive expression of bio energetic organisation. They follow the rhythm of pain and pleasure. Whatever gives pleasure to them they like; whatever gives pain they fight and avoid. Human beings developed a more advanced brain, which allows a more sophisticated expression – the bio psycho energetic language of emotional expression.

If we are in danger, we become afraid. If we are attacked, we get angry. If something is good for us, we are happy. If something hurts us, we are sad. Emotions mobilise our energies and if they are released, our body and mind can relax again. Our nervous system rebalances and allows the natural biological rhythm of contraction and expansion to continue functioning.

If emotions can be released naturally like in a child, we will stay healthy and have an inner balance. The problem begin when morality comes in and we are judged for our emotions: "You should be happy!" "You should not be angry!" "Don't cry!" "Don't be afraid!" We begin controlling ourselves by holding our breath and start to repress a growing mountain of emotions. At any moment, this mountain can explode in an outburst of negativity and make us sick.

If we swallow our anger for years and somebody suddenly provokes us, we are ready to seriously hurt this person. Swallowing our tears for years, we are predestined for depression. If we hide and fight our fear, we may end up in a form of panic attack. If we always try and pretend to be happy by hiding our animosity, we might be closer to a heart attack than we can imagine.

As long as we are unconscious of our emotions in the same way that we are unconscious of our thinking mind, they secretly dominate our life. But if we learn consciously to release our emotional overload, we can avoid negative reactions and live a creative life. We can breathe, relax deeply and enjoy the pleasures of our body. We can have an orgasmic sex life with sensuality and sensitivity.

Sexually repressed people are angry people and having to repress their emotions they also become greedy, depressive and bitter about life. Repressing emotions is like repressing sex. We pervert our emotional life by keeping it unconscious. We don't know any more just how angry, sad, fearful or happy we really are as we forget how sexual we are! We just feel tense!

As a result, we cannot respond consciously to challenging situations anymore because we are afraid that our repressed emotions will overwhelm us and harm others or ourselves. And to a certain extent we are right to be afraid. These repressed emotions have the potential to drive us insane. That's why people who have not learnt to consciously deal with their emotions can end up in a madhouse, hospital or prison. So strong are repressed emotions that they can ruin our life and throw us into the darkest corners of our existence.

In sex, we talk about the extremes of repression and indulgence. As children, we learn to repress our sexual feelings. But the moment we have the chance to live our sex without restrictions, we tend to over indulge. It's either too less or too much without a healthy balance. The same happens in handling our emotions; they are repressed and we hurt ourselves or we overly express them and might hurt others. The art is to find the golden middle.

Trapped in Emotional Repression

Judging, repressing and hiding our emotions keeps us busy by fighting them. We cannot release and we cannot let go of them. We are in a psychological trap. By trying to control them we exhaust our energies and live in permanent stress, causing symptoms like chronic fatigue or depression. To get back our energy for living a positive life, we need to learn to release our repressed emotions.

But why do we learn to repress our emotions in the first place? Most of all we are afraid to lose control and cause chaos in our life. And looking a bit deeper inside ourselves we can also see how afraid we are to feel and to be more vulnerable. We are afraid of our pain and thus repress our pleasure. And we are afraid to feel and see that we might not live the life we long for.

To understand the natural function of emotions is so difficult because they have been manipulated and distorted by layers of harmful conditioning. We have learnt to judge instead of understanding ourselves and the meaning of our emotions. We have learnt to feel guilty for our emotions, which leaves us confused and unable to solve many problems in our life.

The way we are conditioned gives us a pretty narrow interpretation of life and the way it should be. But by definition, interpretations are not the truth and earlier or later they put us in conflict with reality and cause emotional chaos. With this narrow view, we lose a healthy spontaneous emotional response to life and instead get stuck in blind and twisted emotional reactions.

We become afraid of things, which we don't need to be afraid of and relax with things, which are dangerous for us. We are angry in absurd situations and happy about terrible things. Without an awareness of our mental conditioning, we live a distorted emotional life being slaves of our emotions and terrorising each other with our unconscious emotional energies.

For example, a man looks at a woman fascinated by her beauty and she interprets it as somebody wanting sex. Immediately she reacts with great fear or anger. She cannot imagine that somebody just loves to see her. She not only reacts wrongly, she also overreacts. Even if the other wants sex, she could simply say "no" and leave without emotional turmoil.

Being unconscious about our emotional state of being, our life becomes a soap opera full of dramas and intrigues. First we cause a problem by our narrow mindedness and then we try to solve the problem with the same mind that has caused it. We run in a circle, lose our breath and drown in our emotions. Trapped in our emotional mind, we can't find the exit to open the door to our heart.

Inner Liberation by Emotional Release

Once we find a new awareness of our emotions and learn to deal with them consciously, we will have a deep opening for the world of feelings. We will learn to accept our pains and pleasures as a natural and important part of life. We can relax into the flow of life again without being dominated by our unconsciousness.

L. had cancer ten years ago and now it was back. She was ashen-faced, complaining and limping and in total denial of her pain and her needs in this situation. The aggressive return of the cancer probably gave her only a few more months to live. As our work in the group started with her, she avoided every confrontation - physical or psychological - and would collapse and move into passive resistance.

In spite of her resistance, the work with emotional release and deep breathing opened her energetic block. Soon she was able to walk better, even without her walking sticks. Still, she was trapped in the denial of her needs in this situation.

That changed drastically when, one day, the group gave her feedback. Participants shared that they felt she was lying to herself and that she was not accepting the chance that her life gave her in that moment. Finally, her defences broke down and she released her long-repressed pain through a seemingly unending stream of tears. She shared that she always did everything for others, but could not ask for her own needs to be met, or even show them.

Her cancer came back shortly after a colleague betrayed her by stealing and selling the papers for a project she had worked on for years. Around the same time, she was feeling betrayed by her husband, too, who became more interested in pornographic websites than in her.

Now she started to let go of her victim pattern and allowed her rage with those people to be expressed in the group room. She started to stand up for herself and demand that her needs be listened to. I asked her what she would love to do now even if she had only a short time more to live. Clearly - and probably for the first time - she acknowledged her need to enjoy life. Taking a deep breath and with a big smile, she said, "I want to go for a holiday with my husband and I want to renovate my new flat!"

Spontaneously the whole group went to her to take her in their arms. Many participants were touched to tears and sharing how they had the same problem with daring to ask for what they wanted in life. Everybody was impressed by the courage she finally showed in breaking a very old behaviour pattern and taking her last chance to live her desires before it was too late. She started a new relationship with life, with her partner and with herself.

Transforming Emotions

If we release our repressed emotions, consciously we unlock a high amount of potential healing energy into our life stream. A conscious rage attack is hot, like a cleansing fever. A good cry is like a rain shower clearing the air. An outburst of happiness is like an injection of fresh juice into our life. A conscious fear release liberates us from imagined dangers and inner contractions.

All our patterns of emotional reaction show our body-mind reality. The way our ideas and beliefs of life make us think and feel give our body a corresponding structure. In therapy we talk about personality types as a result of our early life conditioning. In short, it means that our personality is not something natural but a distortion of our natural being – our individuality.

Each personality type has a specific unconscious pattern of handling emotions, like cutting off, collapsing, controlling, manipulating, holding or dominating emotions. And all of them correspond with a certain breathing pattern, which is far away from an individual's natural breathing.

Japan, for example, is known as a very rigid society with probably the most controlled people in the world. I have heard that children learn to repress anger by taking some deep breaths, so that they cannot fall into the chaotic breathing pattern of rage.

However, without learning to release the energy of anger, repressing anger has the price of rigidly controlling any spontaneous and joyful expression of life.

An interesting way of dealing with emotions is recorded from Gurdjieff, a mystic living in the first part of the last century. On his deathbed, Gurdjieff's father was teaching him to wait twenty-four hours before expressing anger. Just waiting all this time and being aware of the energy of anger in our body-mind without repressing it, the dark cloud of anger disappears and we can relax again.

But in today's world we are emotionally so overcharged from the stresses of modern life that first we need to discharge ourselves before we are relaxed enough to be able to be aware of our overwhelming emotions. A strong meditative medicine like Osho's *Active Meditations* is needed to release our emotional dramas and transform their energies into love, meditation and celebration.

The Mastering Emotions' Meditation

Repressing emotions is simply unhealthy. Blindly expressing emotions is madness. Consciously releasing emotions is healing. By blocking our heart and repressing emotions, we live mechanically like robots. Opening our heart by releasing repressed emotions, we start feeling and being human again. Ultimately that's the only difference between a robot and a human being – the feeling quality of the heart.

The purpose of releasing our emotional load is to be more peaceful, loving and relaxed. Blocked emotions keep us tense, numb and insensitive to others and ourselves. Liberated from emotional blocks, we become calm and sensitive to the outer and, most importantly, to the inner world too. We are not any more slaves, but masters of our emotions.

Several powerful breathing techniques can help us to transform emotional stress. In the following one we play with our emotions by understanding that each emotion has its own chaotic rhythm of breathing. If we take a moment to imagine our most frequently experienced emotions, we can imagine their breathing pattern too. And we might remember situations when they were overwhelming us.

Vice versa, with our breathing, we consciously can create the chaos of emotions. We can play with them like we can play with our breath. This will help us to take our emotions less seriously, being less afraid of them and stop identifying ourselves with them. If we cease taking our emotional dramas seriously, we can open to the intelligence of the heart as the inner guide for our life.

Stage 1: 10 Minutes Playing with Emotions

Find a space where you can be private. Stand and close your eyes and take a moment to remember different emotional situations from your life before you actually go into playing with them. How did they feel and how did they affect your breathing? Then take a deep breath and let go of them.

Now you will start to imitate different emotions through your breathing and body movements. For imitating each of the emotions, take two to three minutes. Use your breathing to create the emotion and make it so real as if you are an actor who is taken over by his role.

Start with remembering a moment of fear or anxiety and imitate it involving your whole body. Feel how you breathe chaotically in and don't dare to breathe deeply out again. Feel how you hold your breath out of panic that something could happen. Feel the coldness fear brings.

Then remember a moment of anger and play anger as total as you can. Use a chaotic furious breathing, pushing the breath out with only short inhalations. Express the rage with your legs, arms and face. Feel the heat and feel the power of rage!

Next remember a moment of sadness from your life. Your heart is broken. Imitate the crying; imitate the breathing of crying, like broken waves of exhalation and inhalation –

more breathing out than breathing in. Feel the desperation and hopelessness. Feel the pain causing all this sadness.

Finally, remember a moment of happiness. Breathe soft and deep in and out – more in than out! You can't control your overflowing energy. Breathe in delight and feel the high! Keep yourself high so that you cannot fall into the valley of sadness.

Stage 2: 10 Minutes Relaxing

Now sit down comfortably, keep your eyes closed and relax. Let all emotions pass away and let the breathing calm down. Keep your body upright so that you can easily breathe without effort.

Slowly your breathing will relax and you will move beyond the waves of emotions to find inner harmony and peacefulness like a silent lake surrounded by mountains of emotions. Stay relaxed without judging anything. Just remember the breathing coming in and moving out and each breath touching your belly.

Chapter 8

Breathing Into Your Beauty

So shift from thinking to feeling and the best way will be to start breathing from the heart.

Osho

Breathing Like a Child

Let's look at an innocent child, a flower or an animal in wild. What do we see? We see the beauty of creation, the beauty of nature; it touches our heart. It's the beauty of natural breathing!

To compare, let's walk down the street to look at stressed adults following their daily business. Most probably we will see many serious and often sad-looking faces. We will see many people who try to look beautiful by being polite, dressing well, using make-up or even having undergone cosmetic surgery. But we feel that something essential is missing, something that we see in a child; a sense of playfulness, of joy and a natural expression.

What has happened? What happens to the natural beauty of the child so that it changes into a serious and tense adult? What has been lost in the years in between early childhood and adulthood? Simply, the loss of the capacity to breathe deeply and naturally and in such a way that the belly remains soft, the heart opens and the whole being transmits a natural beauty.

73

In addition as a child, our lively, childlike qualities are constantly judged and we are humiliated; therefore we end up feeling that something is wrong with us. We start judging our selves, feeling that we are unintelligent and ugly. Everybody else around us seems to be more beautiful. Even if somebody tells us today that we are beautiful, we cannot believe it. We cannot believe that we are born beautiful – as beautiful as any other living being.

We develop an attitude of putting ourselves down, which manifests in our body, making us feel unattractive. We lose our shiny eyes, our flexible body and our playful expressions. We may suffer from weight problems, or start drinking, or we lose trust in our self as a sexual being. Seeing other people who appear to be more happy and beautiful, we become jealous and frustrated. We lose our breath.

What was natural in the beginning of our life is becoming an effort today – deep, natural breathing. What was once the resource of joy and beauty is becoming the most forgotten part of our life. Now it feels like work to breathe deeply, to feel beautiful and to enjoy ourselves in spite of our stressful lifestyle. In losing our capacity to breathe naturally, we lose the beauty we brought into this life as a newborn child.

And whatever we have not yet lost, we will lose a little more each day with every shallow breath. We age prematurely, lose our spirit for life and become dangerously close to getting seriously sick. We are love, we are beauty and we are trust, but to realise these qualities, to grow and to blossom, we need to learn conscious breathing.

The Healing Power of Loving Our Self

As we do not feel really beautiful and cannot love our self, we are stressed out by all kinds of compensating activities. We please others so that they love us. We try to show to others that we are intelligent, but we don't believe it ourselves. We miss something in ourselves because we have lost the connection with our inner source of beauty, our original being. We desperately try to find on the outside what we miss on the inside.

Our longing for outer beauty and to be attractive is nothing else than the longing to feel our inner beauty and to love ourselves again. No diet, no exercising will have any lasting effect to make us feeling happy if we are missing self-love. We can wear the most beautiful clothes or use the most fragrant perfumes, but nothing will help us to feel the beauty we long for. Without finding our inner beauty, our outer beauty has no foundation and is as fragile as a castle in the sand.

In my years of working with people, I have met many fashion models. What has surprised me the most was to see the discrepancy between their beautiful outlook and their inner feelings regarding themselves. They often feel unworthy and ugly, constantly comparing themselves with other women and criticising their own body as nobody else does.

B. came to our breath and body-oriented therapies and meditations some years ago. Through them she felt happy enough to move on in her life and to try various other spiritual approaches. However, some incidents that weighed heavily on her, along with a growing self-hate brought her back to us. She needed help in reconnecting

75

with her body and to move deeper into the work with herself.

After a long fight within herself, she finally had a breakthrough in a dialogue with her body. She threw out all negative judgments about her body and it revealed to her how it had suffered from being judged and mistreated. The body made it clear that it needed to be taken care of, otherwise it would soon collapse and create more problems for her health. This was a dramatic realisation as she had basically ignored the feelings of her body all her life.

From that day on, she started changing her attitude and began listening to her body carefully. She informs us of her process, of how, since she began to accept her body and to love herself again, she feels more and more beautiful. Through her body she had found a connection to herself again.

Loving ourselves and feeling our beauty starts with loving our body. The moment we accept and respect our body, we can relax and breathe deeply. The body feels acknowledged like an innocent child, which receives the loving attention of its parents. With a fresh breath, our body will invite the vibrant energy of life, this magic elixir that makes us feel shiny and beautiful. In fact, to learn good breathing is the best cosmetic surgery there is to feeling attractive.

The Buddha Belly

With birth we breathe and connect for the first time with this wonderful existence. We feel ourselves as part of it – a new, magnificent, human flower. Our first breath opens our lungs, slowly descends into our belly and we begin to settle in our new body and its fresh spirit. The world looks beautiful because we feel beautiful!

At first, as we enter this new life, we breathe fast, out of the nervousness related to the birth process. We don't know yet if existence will really allow us to enter this new world. But soon our breath begins to relax and supports us with a tremendous flow of life energy. We breathe in and out in harmony with existence, expand into the outer world and connect with all living beings surrounding us.

This deep breath is the resource of our wellbeing. Even if we have forgotten it in the course of our life, we can give rebirth to it at any moment. Opening and exploring the diamond of breath and its energetic potential brings rejuvenation and revitalisation immediately. We can discover what we have always been – a unique and beautiful breath taking flower of existence.

Life is so simple! But our mind likes complicated things and so we miss the ordinary wonders of daily life. That's why we continuously forget to breathe deeply and naturally. It's amazing to realise how easily the feeling of our breathing connects us to feel ourselves as joyful beings. Just feeling our breath and letting it sink all the way down into our belly we come home in ourselves.

For a long time I could not understand why the Japanese Buddha statue has such a big belly. Finally, I understood that it's a symbol of the great energy the Buddha contains, thanks to his deep, relaxed belly breathing. He carries the whole universe in his belly, the source and the richness of life, the thrust into existence, the pleasure of living now and here with totality and a presence in each breath.

The Buddha teaches us that the way to inner richness leads through breathing into our belly. Why then have we forgotten to breathe deep down into our belly? Well, it's because an artificial morality has taught us wrongly to divide life in good and bad instead of learning to accept all aspects of life. So we have learnt for example to judge our sex and to stop belly breathing because it awakens our sexual feelings.

According to religion, there is heaven and hell. We come to heaven when we love the other and be good in terms of society. That means to control ourselves. We go to hell when we are "badly behaving" by following our spontaneous impulses and enjoying the pleasures of our body. Out of fear of being punished, we try to do good things only, but end up doing bad things and feeling guilty.

The Good, the Bad and the Beautiful

The good needs the bad to be good. And the bad needs the good to be bad. If we do not split life into good and bad, both will disappear and give birth to a whole being, which develops a natural morality out of understanding nature and not out of fear. This being will not talk about making love when it means having sex, or talk about good and bad emotions when it is simply afraid of expressing itself.

It will talk about accepting emotions and growing in love. It will accept the belly and its emotions as much as the heart and its sensitive feelings. It will be able to rest in the belly to accumulate the energy for the inner journey towards the heart. Sex is not repressed, emotions are not repressed; it will find the power to trust itself and expand into the flower of love.

We are not aware that the fitness cult around a flat and tense belly has unconsciously grown out of our conditioning to repress and control sex and emotions. In a tense belly, energy gets stuck and causes an ongoing inner pressure, which keeps us hyperactive and stressed. At the same time, young modern fashion keeps the belly free and shows our unconscious longing to see and acknowledge the belly. We just have not found the right way yet to do so.

"Good girls go to heaven, but bad girls go everywhere!" could almost be the slogan of this "showing my belly" fashion. Behind the unconscious longing to reconnect to my belly seems to hide the longing to find an inner home and energetic support for my body, mind, heart and soul to master this fast changing, insecure and exhausting world.

Any artificial moralistic view of life keeps us stuck in our heads and disconnected to our bodies. But being rooted in our belly centre gives us a deep understanding of life and its pleasures. The most moralistic people are getting caught in all kinds of perversions and fall from the holy clouds of morality because of their ignorance of life. Lost in their heads, they have lost the connection to their belly centre and its natural morality.

Missing our belly, we truly miss a decisive part of life. Breathing into our belly, we open to new dimensions in life. We open the centre of life and death, called the Hara in Eastern spiritual traditions, which can give life and take life. We connect to the centre of our inner universe and through it we also connect to the centre of the outer universe.

Loving our belly we can rejoice in a rich life. Missing our belly we miss all that is essential for life.

A Meditation for Belly, Heart and Beauty

Our belly is an all-around star. It allows us to digest food and emotions, nourishes our physical and emotional needs and gives us our sensuality. It accumulates and contains energy and it is a highly sensitive antenna to the vibrations of life surrounding us. Listening to our belly, we have an intuitive insight into life.

Our spiritual journey leads us from the thinking head to the feeling heart and ultimately to the art of being in the belly centre. The belly is a catalyst of our inner growth and makes us feel alive and beautiful. An open belly allows us to stay relaxed in the affairs of our daily life without worry and anxiety. It helps us to be free from the opinions of other people. It is the centre of our life.

We lose our inner balance if we lose our inner centre and without a centre we lose our feeling for the beauty of life. An open belly is like an existential womb welcoming us in to enjoy life. A little meditation can help us to open our belly and experience the beauty of our heart by playing with our breathing. The best is to do the meditation with an empty stomach.

Stage 1: 5 Minutes Connecting to Body and Breath

Stand well grounded with relaxing your knees so that you can feel your feet connecting to mother earth. For a moment, imagine that you are breathing through your feet in and out. If you feel tense shake your tensions out. Come back to imagine breathing through your feet. Allow your body to breathe easily not pushing or holding the breath.

Stage 2: 5 Minutes for Opening Belly and Heart

Now sit down and keep your eyes closed. With the next exhalation pull your belly in and keep your belly muscles contracted as long as possible. When you can't hold it any longer and the urgency for a new inhalation arises, let the belly suddenly relax. Take a deep breath reaching from the belly to the heart. Feel the joy of this new breath opening and connecting your belly and your heart. Feel the lightness it brings to the heart and the beauty it brings to feeling yourself. Repeat the exercise several times.

Stage 3: 5 Minutes Watching the Breath

Stay sitting with closed eyes. Put one of your hands on your belly and the other on your heart. Relax and enjoy the spontaneous movements of your belly breathing. Allow the calmness of your belly to open your heart and touching your whole being, filling it with a feeling of inner beauty.

Stage 4: 5 Minutes Relaxing

Lie down and relax.

Chapter 9

Breathing with the Ocean of Life

There is no beginning and no ending, only a middle. Man is a small wave in the ocean, a small seed full of infinite possibilities.

Osho

The Boy and the Mysterious Ocean

As a boy, I grew up near the Northern Sea. The most beautiful experience was to visit my grandparents who lived on an island surrounded by the stormy waters of the ocean. I loved to play in the dunes, with the winds blowing the sands around me carrying the typical salty smell of the open sea.

No matter how the weather was, I always enjoyed jumping into the ocean, fighting the waves to swim and finally being able to relax into these wild waves. Sometimes I lost my footing and was simply carried away by a strong wave. It was scary, but it was also so exciting. It was mind blowing to experience the unbroken power of nature.

Often I would sit on the shore and watch the ocean. What a feeling just to rest and to allow the vastness of the ocean to touch me. Sometimes a ship would pass by and then again the horizon was empty. Watching this emptiness somehow left a strong and deeply relaxed feeling inside me. It felt as if the ocean was carrying a great secret.

The more I have learnt through the years about water, the more impressed I have become by its mystery. Man has always been fascinated by it; it has been a source of energy and inspiration for artists and poets. The influence that water has in our life is strongly reflected by our language and spiritual traditions.

We use many terms related to water, such as "floating," "letting go," "water-like," "fluid," or "oceanic." Tao follows the "watercourse way," and in Zen enlightenment is described as "the drop disappearing into the ocean," the ego dissolving in the ocean of consciousness. Water is truly a mystic symbol for the natural course of life.

Water is connected to the depths of our unconscious and has a great influence on our feelings and moods. Our biological rhythms are closely attuned to the phases of the moon and the high and low tides of the ocean. The recorded sound of water is used in lots of relaxation and meditation music because it is so soothing for the body and mind.

Water is a female element. It follows gravity when it streams down to earth and always moves in the direction, which gives the least resistance. It is amazingly flexible in finding its way through nature. Water nourishes its surroundings and spreads an atmosphere of tranquillity and safety. Then it is synonymous to an enlightened life style.

Water can also be highly emotional and deadly destructive when it loses its natural balance. It can arrive as a tsunami flooding and destroying cities and also causing the death of people through drowning. This then demonstrates to us the power of blind emotions being expressed without an awareness of its consequences. However, water symbolises life in all its variety from the most peaceful and beautiful to the most dangerous.

Treasures of the Ocean

I am thrilled that today we have finally become aware of the ocean's treasures. In moments when our life is ruled by stress, we may long more and more to cleanse, heal and relax through contact with water; contact with water in the ocean, in a spa, in a hot spring, under a shower, taking a bath, jumping into a river, standing under a waterfall, or drinking from a cool mountain spring.

Water is a unique element. Our body consists mainly of water and the humidity of the air keeps us alive. Body liquids carry the life-supporting gases of breathing to all the nooks and crannies in our body and these liquids also have a cleansing effect in our body.

As a doctor, I learned that the composition of the body's inner milieu is similar to that of the ocean. The extra-cellular space around and between the cells connects the body. It is a kind of internal ocean, one that is sustained by our breath and blood circulation and which cleans, feeds and energises all our body cells.

Water seems to have been a midwife in the formation of stars; water vapour, in the form of interstellar clouds is filling the cosmos. Three quarters of the surface of mother earth consists of water and the human body is just a small replica of the earth.

It is said that our blood consists of ninety-two percent water, our saliva is ninety-eight percent, our bones are twenty-five percent and our organs and brain consist of up to seventy percent. As we have yet to discover and understand the secrets of oceanic waters, we have yet to discover and understand the secrets of our bodily fluids.

Beside the quantity of body liquids and the substances they carry, it is the quality of the water structure and its energetic character that is important. In 1992, Dr Alexis Carrel won the Nobel Prize in medicine for the discovery that the body cell itself is basically immortal. It is the nourishing and cleansing fluid, in which the cell lives, which degenerates and causes the death of the cell.

The physicist, Bell, proved that each atom in the universe is connected to the universe as a whole. This connection occurs through invisible light frequencies. Some protagonists of science claim now that water can be a carrier of information and will also resonate with electromagnetic waves of light. We not only drink water to balance our liquids, but also to receive important information for our wellbeing.

Whirling Waters – Dancing Spirits

One of my most-beloved meditation techniques is the whirling meditation of the Sufi Dervishes. Just moving the body in a circle, as sometimes children playfully do, is energising and enlightening. In fact, whirling is the natural way of water for cleansing and energising itself. In ancient times Incas, Mongolians, Tibetan Monks and the old Greeks of Crete knew this inner alchemy of water.

Wherever water whirls, we find refreshment and rejuvenation. Walking along a riverbed, where water is moving around natural hindrances such as rocks and trees, feels energising. Standing under a waterfall is extremely refreshing and simply looking at whirling and exploding waves in the ocean is electrifying. Jumping into the waves feels like getting rid of an old skin and reconnects us with the freshness of feeling alive. Also, remember the joy of sitting in a whirlpool and being massaged by the whirling waters!

Whirling, moving, dancing and walking are the healthiest activities we can practice for our body, mind, heart and spirit. Sometimes I follow the latest news in medicine. To my delight, I recently read that doctors today are starting to mobilise post-operative patients as soon as possible after their operations in order to help the body recover. This has produced a significant reduction in the number of post-operative deaths.

It helps tremendously to move the fluids of the body and to set in motion the healing power of water; as long as water moves, the energy moves, but once water gets stuck, energy gets stuck and the doors are open to dis-ease.

Children like to dance and run in the rain, to play in a pond or play on the beach; we hear them screaming with pleasure and enjoying the energetic atmosphere around water. Children are more connected to the ocean waters because not long ago they were still growing in the inner ocean of the mother's womb; they were living like fish in the deep sea – relaxed and happily floating and growing into life.

Aquaprana Ocean Healing

My exciting experiences with water motivated me to work with its healing and rejuvenating powers, permitting me to have a much deeper understanding of my work as a physician and as a breath therapist.

Floating, relaxing and breathing in the ocean is not only healthy for physical and emotional healing, it also fulfils our spiritual longing to move beyond the narrowness of the mind and the problems this narrowness causes. It allows us to have a feeling of the limitless ocean of existence and the unbelievable easiness of being.

The ocean inspired me to develop the work of *Aquaprana Ocean Healing*. Aqua means water and Prana means life energy contained in the breath. Opening our breath in the presence of the ocean is tremendously healing and rejuvenating. We learn to move with the spontaneous flow of life to what is known in Tao as "the watercourse way."

This work is a gentle, therapeutic method to unwind, release and dissolve chronic physical or emotional tensions accumulated through all the different stages of life, beginning with our pre-natal existence. Warm water acts as a therapeutic womb where a partner moves us and reconnects us to the self-healing stream of our life energy.

Soft breathing combined with body and energy work in warm water allows us to overcome severe stress symptoms and psychological conflicts. Many of our fears and traumas are related to water. The fear of letting go or losing control especially is often seen in people who are afraid of water.

Capitalising on the female qualities of water the work of *Aquaprana Ocean Healing* gives back to us our natural vulnerability and sensitivity by gently reconnecting and releasing our old pains and feelings of hurt. This is why this therapy can be so healing, not only for ourselves, but also for our relationships.

By dominating and conquering nature, we have lost our trust in nature and ourselves. The beauty of this work is to see how easily we can learn to trust again, by simply permitting somebody to move us through the waves of the ocean. Floating on top of soft waves, or being guided underwater by the therapist, reconnects us to primordial life and connects us with the origin of life on earth. It is an experience that can change our life profoundly.

Waves of Energy – Waves of Trust

I have loved the Caribbean Sea from the time I was invited for the first time to visit the island of Los Roques, which is part of a huge coral reef in front of Venezuela. Later on, I met the same quality in the ocean at the Riviera Maya in Mexico.

What makes it so special is the white sand and the wonderful tropical climate, with hours of sun and sometimes light, refreshing showers. It is full of palms and mangrove forests, but most impressive is the turquoise ocean water. Just taking a swim and then floating on the salty warm ocean waves is a rejuvenating treat in itself.

Once a friend sent me a beautiful letter of love from the Caribbean:

"I love listening to the waves of the ocean or feeling the waves touching me, penetrating my protections and melting my contractions. I cool down, relax and feel that I am expanding with the ocean. I start closing my eyes and become lighter feeling the pleasure of the smooth ocean breeze gently touching my skin.

I feel a longing to become part of this beautiful ocean. Nature plays a wonderful symphony and I like to be part of it.

I am ready to jump into the sea, diving into the waves and feeling the water all around me playing the song of life. Finally turning around on my back and floating on the soft warm waves of the Caribbean is a great experience of letting go. I forget time and space and it feels like disappearing in eternity. This very moment is divine; this very ocean feels like paradise! Waves of acceptance touch my heart and everything feels right the way it is. It feels like meditation!

Coming out of the water I like to relax and carry this beautiful experience of letting go with me. I close my eyes and still feel the vibration of the ocean inside. A deep peacefulness descends on me. Something relaxes so deeply inside that it seems as if I am touching the silence of the universe. It feels as if I am touching the inner ocean of life – of myself."

The Ocean Wave Meditation

The Ocean Wave Meditation is a beautiful device for playing and connecting with the nature of water and with the nature of being. We learn to let go and breathe deeply, to enjoy our body, become flexible, refresh our spirits and relax into our inner being. We become "spiritual aquanauts" diving into our inner ocean, where we can find peace and harmony and a growing acceptance of our life.

Whenever we forget the feeling of expansion, the feeling of connectedness with nature and joyful living, or when we simply wish to share a great experience with a partner, we can do this meditation alone or together. We can reconnect to the inner ocean wherever we are and with whomever we are. The ocean can always be with us reminding us of the mystery of life.

In this meditation we first play like the waves in the ocean. We reach to the peaks and to the valleys of the wave feeing the energy moving us. In fact, the movement of a wave is present throughout our body; our blood is pulsing like waves through our entire circulatory system, our breathing comes in waves all over our body, our intestines move in the waves of peristalsis and our moods come in waves of ups and downs.

Beneath all the movement on the surface of the ocean there is deep silence in its very depth. But once in a while, the surface of the ocean also becomes very calm and peaceful, feeling similar to when the mental waves of thoughts and emotions relax and we settle into a deep meditative state of being.

The best time for this meditation is at night and it is very helpful to listen to ocean music like in my *Ocean Love Meditation* for support.

Stage 1: 10 Minutes Moving and Breathing Like a Wave

Find a place to stand or kneel on your knees. Now start becoming like a wave; begin with slowly breathing in and stretching the arms slowly upward towards the sky with open eyes and open mouth. Stretch out as far as possible, until the body is completely extended, your palms and face turning upwards to let the wave come to its peak.

Pause for a moment. Feel the amount of energy you contain and hold your breath for as long as it is comfortable.

Then close your eyes, breathe slowly out and allow your body to lower itself gently to the ground, with your forehead touching the earth. Stretch out your hands and arms so that they rest on the ground. With your exhalation sink deeply into the valley of the wave and let go of everything so that you become totally empty. For a moment, rest and feel yourself surrendering to existence.

Then slowly rise up again like a wave and move upwards as before. Just as a wave does, you rise high and you fall deep down. Just as a wave does you are disappearing into the ocean – the ocean of existence. Slowly you will become like the waves; you will feel like the waves and even hearing the sound of the waves.

Stage 2: 10 Minutes Relaxing in the Ocean of Life

With eyes closed, lie on your back and rest. Feel your breathing relaxing and becoming silent; soon you will feel a deep relaxation and a great peacefulness descending on you. The ocean becomes silent, the waves of the mind disappear and you disappear.

Doing this meditation at night you may simply let go into sleeping and enjoying a rejuvenating rest.

Chapter 10

Breathing in Love and Meditation

Let love be like breathing. Breathe in, breathe out, but let it be love coming in, going out. By and by, with each breath, you have created the magic of love.

Osho

The Journey from Fear to Love

In many aspects, our life is a journey from fear to love. First we need to overcome our fears for survival before we are able to discover the spirit of love. Our education does not teach us how to enjoy a fearless life and does not give us the courage to be our self, moving happily with change and insecurity; change and insecurity are the nature of life. In fact, our education has a higher value of safety than the art of living, loving and laughing!

If we get stuck in fear we cannot grow in love. The river of life's energy gets blocked before it can reach to our heart. Whatever we do, we remain orientated on survival and material affairs. Money, prestige and success become substitutes for love, preventing us from growing into a compassionate human being. Jealousy, competition, boredom and frustration begin to rule our life. We miss the flowering of life because we miss love.

As a physician I could see how fear leads to tension, chronic contraction and disease. The fear of life makes us sick, depressive or suicidal. The inability of living our energy independently from the judgments of others keeps us imprisoned in a cage of anxiety and restlessness. We live like a tiger in a zoo – civilised but deprived and afraid of our freedom.

During my life, I am happy to have discovered the power of breath as a great tool to transform my fears of life and explore the world of love, death and meditation. These are beautiful and existential teachers in the most electrifying experience of life; the art of letting go. In love, I learn to let go of my mind and in death I learn to let go of my body. Meditation finally is both, an experience of letting go of all our identifications with body and mind.

In the centre of my life and I guess for many of you, is a seemingly endless search for love. We look for someone who loves us and we long to feel more loving. With each relationship where we experience our limited ability to love, comes a longing for inner freedom – to feel free from all the limitations we put on the beauty of love.

A friend in midlife crisis once told me: "I'm getting so tired of my angry, fearful or depressive reactions when I get rejected. I cannot relax anymore and feel lonely, betrayed, ignored and humiliated. And I am so tired of making compromises in my relationship when I want some space to feel free and my partner stops me. I am tired of all my emotional reactions and projections. I love my partner, but what has all this to do with love? I am confused!"

Yes, there comes a point in our life, when we ask ourselves what life is all about. We do our job, we have money and we are somehow successful. We have a normal relationship with all the problems most relationships have - moments of intimacy alternating with intense fights, jealousy, competition, demands or rejections. We are together, but often we feel lonely at the same time. All in all, life starts feeling like an empty routine.

Well, this scenario can be a great wake-up call for us and might be the beginning of a great change in our life. We start looking for a new way of being and a path to find the meaning of life. We might be afraid of our inner transformation, but we also know that living the compromise of being half alive and half dead is deeply frustrating.

Sooner or later, we will realise that we have to face and overcome our fears of living the life we long for – a life where we can grow by the healing power of love into inner freedom and creativity.

Love Prevents Madness

Have you ever observed mad people consciously? They live in their own world disconnected from society. In their own way they are free, but it is a freedom in inner isolation. Their fear of life keeps them unconscious and the joy to expand into the world of love seems closed. Opening the locked door to love in a safe environment is their greatest longing and in fact could be their healing.

In different ways we might all have felt the fear of going crazy. But knowing the power of love prevents us from it. Love gives us an inner security and connectedness to the world. We have an inner centre; we trust ourselves and we are not afraid to lose mental control because we are rooted in a much stronger force – our heart. We can even laugh and play with our madness without getting serious about it.

In working with schizoid people – people who have a tendency to split from reality under stress – I have learned that the tendency towards madness often goes back to a life-threatening trauma in prenatal life. A mother lost a close relative, tried an abortion, had an accident, got beaten by the husband or tried suicide and transmitted this threatening experience to the unborn in her belly.

Here the most intimate experience of being in the womb of our mother became terribly threatening. Sadly, these kinds of early life experiences can leave us with a deep fear of being intimate and feeling connected to life. Then mistrust, paranoia, attacking or pushing people away seems to be the only possible way to survive and to come close to people feels dangerous.

Yes, pregnant mothers today are exposed to the many stresses and fearful situations of modern life. Working, home care, social duties or being exposed to a lot of environmental pollution, gives them no time to breathe or to relax. The unborn develops under the influence of permanent stress and it's not surprising that later on the youngster suffers from hyperactivity, violence, drug abuse or even suicidal tendencies.

Being lost in a mental world, we all carry a certain degree of madness. We live in our own secluded universe of ideas, morality and beliefs. We feel afraid to trust and cannot relate to others with an open heart. We keep ourselves protected from life and keep on running and running until we finally break down. We don't realise how crazy we are already and each day pulls us deeper into madness!

The level of anxiety in modern societies is alarming and instead of pills we need a new culture of lovingness. Not knowing the power of our spiritual heart and living a mentally dominated life is simply too dangerous. Any big shock at any moment in our life can throw us from our thin layer of consciousness into the darkness of the unconscious where nobody can reach us anymore.

Love Heals the Fear of Orgasm

Repression of sex is repression of nature and leads to the destruction of nature. If we can't even enjoy loving our own body anymore, how can we love and care for nature? However well meant our morality might be, it has been learnt and therefore an artificial product of our mind. It does not come naturally with birth; it comes with mental conditioning.

Morality gives us a safe feeling that we know life. But this is an illusion because life is unpredictable and there is no way to put it into a formula. We create a morality to organise our life, but it becomes harmful when this morality runs our life and stops us discovering our inner nature.

A joyful life needs a deep understanding of our nature as human beings and this starts with our sex energy. Oh yes, we seem to be much more open to sex today. We openly talk about it, but still might turn off the lights when being naked for making love. However, hesitantly we begin to accept our animal nature. But are we getting more loving in our sex life and do we know about its spiritual dimension?

Yes, sex is more available; but what about the quality? If our sex energy cannot flow towards our heart and open a new dimension of love, it will become more frustrating and abusive. Just to enjoy sex for the sheer pleasure of it seems often difficult. We are so used to connecting sex with reproduction that sooner or later we end up giving birth to a child, adding to an already dangerously exploding over population.

Why is it so dangerous? It is so dangerous because overpopulation exhausts the resources and ultimately leads to the destruction of our environment. Out of compassion for our beautiful nature, we should give to mother earth only as many children as she can nourish and give space to.

A child is beautiful, but should not be created to make us happy. Out of our own joy for life, we should be able to make him or her happy, otherwise it's better not to have children. There are so many other and more advanced ways to be creative. But they all need a deep acceptance of our sex energy, because liberating this basic energy is the beginning of creating a truly rich life. And the deep acceptance of sex leads to nature's highest expression – orgasm. In orgasm biology meets spirituality.

Orgasm is an indicator for the depth of our sex life, our relating and the state of our health. It's the peak experience of sex and can transform our life. It is not a social category and neither related to family issues or the creation of children. It's purely egoistic and at the same time the most non-egoistic and connecting experience to support social life. It brings joyfulness, harmony and peacefulness into our world!

I would like to mention a little anecdote about some scientists who went out to observe the life of the bonbon monkey. The scientists were expecting the usual "monkey business" of fighting and competition for the leadership of the tribe, but to their surprise they saw the monkeys solving their conflicts through all kind of sexual activities – women with men, women with women, men with men.

Missing orgasm brings frustration; enjoying orgasm brings bliss. It is a religious experience and lifts us beyond the limitations of our body and mind, of space and time. For a moment we feel like a free energy being one with the universe. It's a moment of great lightness and leaves us with an incredible gratefulness to our partner. It is a gratefulness that opens our heart.

The problem is that we have learnt to feel safe only if we can control everything and orgasm can only happen if we don't control ourselves. In orgasm, we need to be able to let go of all life's education and social conditioning. Only a trusting space can open us for the beauty of letting go of control and disappearing into orgasm.

Fear deprives our sex of orgasm and blocks its transformative power. But a loving attitude towards life allows us to make orgasm a stepping-stone into the world of no-mind – the world of meditation. Love heals our fear of orgasm and the fear of us humans to live an orgasmic life style. It is like a small death that opens us for a greater life.

Love Transforms Death

Once in a meditation orientated therapy group for healing childhood relationships, a friend shared with us that she often feels anxiety during the night and cannot have a good night's sleep. In her therapeutic process she remembered that in her childhood, during the night, her parents were often fighting. Her father wanted to have sex, but her mother refused and called him a pervert. This started when her mother was pregnant with her.

Then she told us an interesting dream: While she was home with her daughter one night, she heard people trying to break into her house. They were the same people who usually worked during the day as gardeners around her house. She was very scared and tried to hide herself and her daughter. While the people broke into the house, she desperately tried to find a way to get out of this threatening situation.

Four solutions came to her mind; the first was to try to escape, the second to call the police, the third to be killed and the fourth to love. As the first three ideas seemed hopeless, she decided to go for the fourth, to try it with love. Then she woke up – her unconscious had provided her with a splendid solution. She realised that love instead of fighting or collapsing was the solution to many problems in her life, which were connected to the fearful relationship with her father.

In some therapy groups, I work with a structure to say goodbye to a beloved one who has died or separated from us. Usually it confronts participants with immense emotional pain. In this process of consciously letting go of the body of the other, they realise something very important. They experience that the body is born and that the body dies, but a beautiful space of lovingness with the other remains and this feels eternal.

It is true; real love never seems to die because it is not of the body and not of the mind. It is of the soul. It allows us to forgive whatever has hurt us or will hurt us. It is like the spirit of existence, liberating us from all fear and tension and pain, which we have collected in the course of our life. Wherever there is love, we can relax, trust and let go into the unknown.

Sometime ago, my brother died unexpectedly because of a badly treated tooth infection, which spread into the heart and the whole body. For weeks he was in a coma and his body looked decimated. As he was not conscious, I could not converse with him, but I spent some time sitting beside him, breathing with him, feeling him and sharing with him what I wanted to let him know as a brother. Somehow I felt he could hear me.

It was the last moment we spent together in this lifetime. I shared my love and my understanding for his situation and I told him that if he needed to leave this life and his family, it would be okay and we would find a way to support his family. After a moment of being slightly agitated, his breathing relaxed again and we shared a deep silence and connectedness. I am sure that he understood and I still carry this beautiful moment of understanding with me.

Yes, love heals even the fear of death and allows us to pass peacefully into another dimension of life. In India I learnt to accept death as part of life because it is not hidden and is present in many ways. Even the burning gates are public and I attended some cremations to confront myself with the reality of death. In being with dying friends, I experienced the transformative power of love.

With the death of my brother, I realised that love and lightness never die. In fact, the other leaving us can be a great gift in teaching us that in the end only the ability to love counts. If we don't learn the art of love, we waste our life. We cry in the face of death because we realise that we did not live intensely enough to find the diamond of love in our life.

Love Needs No Middleman – Love Needs You

The true experience of love is between existence and me. As children we learn that we have to love our parents to survive. When we grow up, we learn to love our partner for fulfilling our needs for intimacy. When we grow wise, we learn to love for loves sake! We travel along the river of love from being totally dependent on others, to love providing us with ultimate inner freedom.

All our love relationship experiences can sharpen our intelligence and allow us to grow a little more. Nobody can tell us what love is until we realise it ourselves. Love is not a moral category, but an experience of our connectedness with existence. No middleman is needed to tell us what love is. Any idea of love will only stop our search for it because it gives us the illusion that we know it already. Love cannot be taught, but can be invited by our courage to walk through the fire of life.

In school I was pretty interested in the teachings of different religions. But once, when a priest demanded that we should be grateful to God and our parents because they teach us love, I had to laugh and got thrown out of the classroom. I was just thinking; the slaughters of the Second World War are just over, my parents fight more than love each other and the priest throws me out of the classroom just because I don't take him seriously. What kind of love can these people teach me?

I had to realise that they teach suffering and seriousness in the name of love. Instead of loving ourselves as alive, sensual, breathing and humorous individuals, they want us to follow and believe in their ideas of love. It's really amazing that we learn everything in school except the most important thing for a fulfilling life – the art of love and enjoying ourselves.

That is why we desperately "hunt" for love in God, in our relationships, or in our family and still miss it. We cannot find in the outside world what is a quality of our inner world. Love is waiting inside us and there we can discover it. That is the whole purpose of meditation.

The Magic of Love Meditation

A good breath cleans, oxygenates and energises our body and keeps us healthy. It also carries the energy to open our heart for the experience of love. Love grows out of rich life experience and the deeper our life is related to a good breath, the easier love happens. In fact, love is our inner breath and it should be as natural as our breathing. Now we come to the meditation.

Stage 1: 5 Minutes Shaking and Breathing to Release Stress

Stay standing; keep your feet well grounded and your knees flexible. Shake out all your tensions, open your mouth and breathe deeply so that you are prepared to go into the meditation more fresh and relaxed.

Stage 2: 5 Minutes Feeling the Rhythm of Breath

Find a place to sit down comfortably, relax and close your eyes. For a moment observe your breathing. While inhaling, feel the expansion of your body and while exhaling, feel the relaxation. Each breath is connecting you with the breath of life. Expansion and relaxation, opening and letting go are the heartbeat of existence. Feel the breath being the eternal rhythm of life.

Stage 3: 5 Minutes Expanding in Love

Now allow the opening of your heart by the diamond of breath. While staying connected to your breathing, slowly rest your hands in the middle of your chest. Gently breathe into the area of your heart and imagine the aura of your spiritual heart surrounding your physical heart.

Allow the breathing to nourish your spiritual heart and imagine that you radiate love. Let it expand from your heart centre in all directions of your body. Then let it further expand all around your body like an invisible aura. Start filling the room with love energy and keep on expanding into the area outside the room – the house, the city and the country you are living in.

Finally, love expands all around mother earth and fills the whole universe. All becomes love and love becomes all. Feel and breathe with the vibrations of delightful energy all around you. Feel being part of it and enjoy relaxing into the art of being. Allow the body to swing as if moved by gentle waves in the ocean of love.

Stage 4: 5 Minutes Relaxing in Love

Lie down and stay with closed eyes. Relax in the beautiful atmosphere you have created with love surrounding you. For so long you have searched for love everywhere and now you find it in and all around yourself. Love has become your inner breath. Love is becoming your meditation.

About the Author

Throughout all the phases of my life, from being a small child to being an athlete, an artist, a rebel, a physician and a therapist, I have always felt the longing for love, joy and health.

For more than thirty years now as a therapist on the path of transformation, conscious breathing has become my best friend in my life long search for love, freedom and creativity. It has given me strength and inspiration on my journey from fear to love and from sex to meditation; it is a journey into the mystery of life.

I was born in 1951 in the north of Germany and in the late seventies after completing my studies in medicine at the University of Kiel, I started working as a medical doctor. I very quickly realised that the underlying cause of many diseases can be found in unresolved psychological conflicts, blocked energy flow and an unfulfilled spiritual longing. This encouraged me to gain further education in body-psychotherapy, breath work, encounter and primal therapy in the context of individual, group and communal therapy.

In 1979, I met the enlightened mystic Osho and became initiated into meditation. After years of searching for the meaning of life, meditation finally gave me the first delightful experience of the inner world. It gave me the courage to be myself, to trust life and to search not for more knowledge, but to find an experiential knowing. All this has changed my life and, as a result, transforming the quality of life became the principle focus of my personal and professional being.

I left traditional medicine to focus on preventative healing methods and spiritual therapy. I was the founder of two different growth centres in the '80s, one in Berlin and the other in Munich and I also became the director of the Center for Transformation in the Osho Commune in Pune, India, a position I held for several years.

I was invited to introduce my work to various institutions, including the University of Berlin (Germany), the University of San Diego (USA), TATA Management School (India), Deloitte Touch Tohmatsu (Mexico), Tennis Australia and also to the general public through various conferences, radio and TV programmes.

Today, I am the director of the *Osho International Breath Energy School*, teaching the work of *Osho Diamond Breath.* Here, modern scientific insights into bio-energy, breath therapy, emotional healing and human psychology merge with modern spirituality and the teachings of ancient mystery schools, working towards a new psychology; a Psychology of the Buddha.

In today's stressed society, partnerships often miss a deep understanding and sharing of love, trust and intimacy. Growing in love and meditation in a friendly environment is an urgent need for all of us. Based on my rich experiences in relating – personal, professional and in communal life – I have developed a process for *Healing Relationships*; this process is greatly supported by deep breath work.

As a small boy, I was fascinated by the wild ocean and enjoyed sitting at the beach contemplating the secrets of life. As an adult, I was invited to the warm Caribbean Sea, where I became aware of the healing potential of nature.

With *Aquaprana Ocean Healing* I discovered a soft therapy for relaxing, trusting and letting go into our inner ocean of peace and blissfulness.

The Tantric way of energy transformation and the Zen approach of presence, playfulness and paradox are keys in my work with people. These keys allowed me to create a process called *Life-Line De-conditioning*, which brings the healing power of awareness to the various phases of our life, liberating us from chronic stress patterns. Healing in love and growing in meditation are the secrets of Osho's *Spiritual Therapy*.

Seeing young children staying healthy and being innocent because of their natural state of playfulness, inspired me to develop the *Zen Wind – Zen Play Meditations*. It's an approach to rediscover our childlike innocence for inner healing using the art of meditation.

Together with a team of therapist friends, I created the *Summer Multiversity* in the heart of Italy's beautiful Tuscany. Each year this three-month programme of inner growth, therapy and transformation training, takes place in the *Osho Miasto Commune*, which is surrounded by the wonders of nature. This is a period of time-out for healing ourselves, for intimate meetings with friends from around the globe and for gaining important insights into a new way of living.

Information about Devapath's work:

http://www.diamondbreath.com
http://www.devapath.info

www.ingramcontent.com/pod-product-compliance
Lightning Source LLC
LaVergne TN
LVHW021352080426
835508LV00020B/2242